U0799852

LINGNAN CULTURE
YOUTH BOOK

岭南文化青年读本

STARTING FROM GUANGZHOU

从广州出发

上册

共青团广州市委员会 编

南方日报出版社
NANFANG DAILY PRESS
中国·广州

图书在版编目（CIP）数据

岭南文化青年读本. 上册 / 共青团广州市委员会 编. -- 广州 : 南方日报出版社, 2019.10
ISBN 978-7-5491-2081-9

Ⅰ. ①岭… Ⅱ. ①共… Ⅲ. ①地方文化－广东－青年读物 Ⅳ. ①G127.65-49

中国版本图书馆CIP数据核字（2019）第223543号

LINGNAN WENHUA QINGNIAN DUBEN
岭南文化青年读本（上册）

编　　者：共青团广州市委员会
出版发行：南方日报出版社
地　　址：广州市广州大道中289号
出 版 人：周山丹
责任编辑：刘志一　李佳航
封面设计：肖晓文
责任技编：王　兰
责任校对：魏智宏
经　　销：全国新华书店
印　　刷：广州岭美文化科技有限公司
开　　本：889mm×1194mm　1/32
印　　张：4.5
字　　数：210千字
版　　次：2019年10月第1版
印　　次：2019年10月第1次印刷
定　　价：68.00元（全两册）

投稿热线：（020）87360640　　读者热线：（020）87363865

前　言

岭南文化作为中华优秀传统文化的有机组成部分，基于独特的地理环境和历史条件，在发展过程中不断吸取和融会中原文化和海外文化，逐渐形成自身独有的特点。岭南人开放的思想、务实的作风、创新的精神、兼容并蓄的胸怀，使得岭南文化呈现大气磅礴的形态，更适宜在新时代发展和传承。

2018年10月，习近平总书记视察广州时，就十分关心岭南非物质文化遗产的保护、传承与发展工作，提出“要注重文明传承、文化延续，让城市留下记忆，让人们记住乡愁”，明确要求广州要实现老城市新活力，在综合城市功能、城市文化综合实力、现代服务业、现代化国际化营商

FOREWORD

As one integral part of the excellent traditional Chinese culture, Lingnan culture that is always ready to absorb and integrate the cultures of Central China and overseas cultures in the process of its development while taking the unique geography and history of Lingnan as its root has formed its unique features. Lingnan people with an open, inclusive mind and pragmatic, innovative spirit have created for Lingnan culture an image of sublime magnificence and provide good opportunities for its development and dissemination in the new era.

In Oct, 2018, when General Secretary Xi Jinping visited Guangzhou, he showed great interest in the protection, dissemination and development of Lingnan intangible cultural heritages. He poined out that we should pay attention to the inheritance of civilization and the continuation of culture, so that the city can revive its memories and people can evoke their nostalgia. Guangzhou is clearly required to realize the new vitality of the old city and make new achievements in the comprehensive urban functions, comprehensive strength of urban culture,

环境方面出新出彩。

当前，“一带一路”倡议正在加快实施，岭南文化的传承传播也恰逢其时。广州是岭南文化的重要发源地。组织编撰《岭南文化青年读本》一书，是共青团广州市委为繁荣本土文化，立足岭南文化，努力讲好中国故事、传递中国声音的一次积极作为，也是加强青年教育以及青年文化阵地建设的一次积极尝试。做好岭南文化在当代的传承发展，需要全社会的共同努力，更需要青年参与到对岭南文化的认知和认同上来。

为了让读本更生动，传播范围更广泛，我们将本书分为上下两册，以图文并茂、中英双语的形式，通过简洁的文字和丰富的图片，向青年普及岭南文化的六个方面：岭南画派、广东音乐、粤剧、岭南建筑、岭南民俗以及粤菜。上册主要介绍“岭南三秀”——岭南画派、广东音乐及粤剧，这三者是岭南文化中最具代表性和革新精神的文艺形态。下册则涵盖了岭南人民的生活细节，从岭南建筑、岭南民俗和粤菜这三个方面，体现岭南文化兼收并

modern service industry and modern international business environment.

At present, "the Belt and Road" Initiative has already started. And Lingnan culture is provided with a good opportunity for rapid development. Guangzhou is an important birthplace of Lingnan culture. Guangzhou Municipal Committee of Communist Youth League, focusing on Lingnan culture, organized the production of the book *Lingnan Culture: Youth Book*, aiming to develop the local culture, telling Chinese stories and letting the world hear China's voice. It is also a positive trial to reinforce the cultural and ideological education among the young people. The development of Lingnan culture in the new era needs the contribution of the whole society, especially the young generation's understanding and recognition of Lingnan culture.

We divide this book into two volumes to help the readers enjoy the beauty and vitality of Lingnan culture and also to atrract more readers. It uses concise language and a great variety of pictures to introduce the young readers to six sections of Lingnan culture in both Chinese and English, including Lingnan painting, Cantonese music, Cantonese opera, Lingnan architecture, Lingnan customs and Cantonese delicacy. Volume One mainly focuses on the "three treasures of Lingnan", that is Lingnan painting,

蓄、开放包容、务实敢为的特质。

本书为青年打开了一扇了解岭南文化的窗，我们希望广大青年能够通过本书，从艺术成就与生活日常入手触摸岭南文化精神特质，感受岭南文化的独特魅力，激发他们传承和弘扬岭南文化的责任感、使命感。我们更希望这本书可以“走出去”，促进不同文明之间的互联互通、互学互鉴、交流对话、和谐共生。

新时代，新气象，新作为，愿本书能够为岭南文化继续彰显展示独特优势，充满信心走向世界尽一份绵薄之力。

Cantonese music and Cantonese opera which are the most innovative and representative forms of Lingnan culture. Volume Two focuses on the everyday life of Lingnan people, including Lingnan architecture, Lingnan customs and food which embody the inclusive, open, practical and innovative qualities of Lingnan culture.

This book opens a new window for young people whoever wants to understand the essence of Lingnan culture. We hope they can touch Lingnan culture through artistic achievements and daily life of Lingnan people, feel the charm of Lingnan cultrue by this book, urge them to take up the mission to inherit and develop Lingnan culture. And we also hope that this book can "go out" to facilitate the communication and exchange between different world civilizations for the construction of a harmonious society.

New era, new challenge, new trial! We hope this book will contribute to the exhibition of the glamour of Lingnan culture before the whole world.

目 录

CONTENTS

综 述

岭南，北枕五岭，南濒大海，宏大壮阔。

从地理概念上看，背靠重叠险峻的南岭山脉；斜倚连绵不绝的海岸线，面向浩瀚海洋。自秦始皇统一岭南后，先进的中原文化逐步南移。特别是历史上几次大的移民潮，岭南地区都成为南下移民的最后归宿地。来自五湖四海的移民群带来的中原文化，在岭南特殊的自然条件与社会条件下与原有的土著文化不断碰撞、吸收、融合，交流融汇，生根发芽，进一步丰富了岭南文化的内容。而自汉唐以来，岭南地区一直是中国历史上重要的对外贸易基地，海上贸易打开与世界文化交流的天窗。这种根植中华文化，对外来文化兼收众长、皆为我用的气度促使岭南文化形成开放、务实、兼容、创新的特征。

OVERVIEW

The vast land called Lingnan borders with the five ridges in the north and faces the vast blue in the south.

Geographically, Lingnan region uses the gorgeous Lingnan ridges as the barrier. In the south, it borders with the vast sea along the endless coastline. After Qin Shi Huang, the first emperor of a unified China, united Lingnan region, the developed cultures of Central China moved here and gradually took their roots in this region. Several large-scale immigrations in the history of China turned Lingnan into the home of countless northerners. These immigrants brought with them the cultures of Central China which clashed with and merged into the local culture in this region to fit the special social and natural environment here and enriched Lingnan culture. Since Han and Tang dynasties, Lingnan had always been one important place for China's trading with merchants from other countries. The world trade going on here opened the gate for Lingnan culture's communication with the world cultures. Rooted in the traditional cultures of China while absorbing foreign ones,

习近平总书记指出：“文化同国运相牵，文脉同国脉相连。”“中国特色社会主义文化，源自于中华民族五千多年文明历史所孕育的中华优秀传统文化。”国家和民族的强盛，是以文化的发展兴盛为根基的。

习近平总书记对广东提出“四个走在全国前列”的寄语，在广州视察时也提出城市文明传承和根脉延续十分重要，传统和现代要融合发展。岭南文化作为中华民族优秀传统文化的重要组成部分，经过两千多年的锤炼演变，已经渗透到岭南社会、经济和精神生活各个领域，成为影响岭南地区历史发展的强大力量，为岭南地区的自身发展及其与东南亚各国的合作发展提供了巨大助力。

Lingnan culture formed its special features that proved to be open, practical, inclusive and innovative.

General Secretary Xi Jinping points out: "Culture is always connected with the national prosperity, and the development of a culture is connected with its mother country." "The socialist culture with Chinese characteristics originates from the outstanding traditional Chinese culture nurtured by the more than 5000 years of civilization of China." The prosperity of a nation is rooted in the prosperity of its culture.

General Secretary Xi Jinping puts forward the hope of "gain four leads nationally" for Guangdong, and also points out that it is very important to inherit urban civilization and continue its roots during the investigation in Guangzhou. Traditional and modern development should be integrated. After 2000 years' development, Lingnan culture, an important part of the traditional culture of China in general, has penetrated into every corner of Lingnan politics, economy and spiritual life, has become a force that may influence the history of Lingnan region, and has led to the profound development Lingnan and its communication with Southeast Asia.

In the history of China, Guangzhou which is the center of Lingnan culture, was the starting point of the Maritime Silk Road, the meeting ground of the eastern and the western cultures. It can be said that Guangzhou occupied a very important position in the history of cultural

在历史上，岭南文化的中心地广州是海上“丝绸之路”的起点、东西方文化交流的门户，在中西文化相互融合方面有着举足轻重的地位。

在经济上，作为改革开放的领头羊，珠三角经济在全国排名前列，经济发展为岭南文化发展提供物质保障。

在文化上，2017年“粤港澳大湾区”正式写入政府工作报告，将建成以中华文化为主流、多元文化共存的交流合作基地。岭南文化作为粤港澳同宗同源的文化，有强大的凝聚力，对推动粤港澳大湾区的经济发展和文化建设起到了润滑催化的作用。

communication between the east and the west.

Economically, as the leading force of the economic opening policy in China, the economy of Pearl River Delta stays at the top place of Chinese economy. Its economic advantages provide material support for the development of Lingnan culture.

In 2017, Guangdong–Hong Kong–Macao Greater Bay Area was written into China's governmental report. It will be established as the platform for the cultural communication between China and the world. Lingnan culture is a culture shared by Guangdong, Hong Kong and Macao, and its cohesive force will promote the economic and cultural development in the Greater Bay Area.

In terms of overseas dissemination, Lingnan culture enjoys rich resources provided by the multitude of overseas Chinese. The people of Guangdong had a tradition since the ancient time to earn their living in other countries. There are now about 30 million Cantonese-speaking overseas Chinese from Guangdong, about a half of all the overseas Chinese. As a cultural link, Lingnan culture helps unite the Chinese people all over the world, and promotes the cultural communication between China and the world.

Lingnan culture is a composition of the tangible as well as intangible cultural forms created by Lingnan people in their harmonious communication with the nature. It encompasses the cultural value and thinking or

在海外传播上，海外华侨资源丰厚。粤人自古有下南洋谋生的传统，海外粤籍侨胞约3000万人，占全国海外侨胞总数一半以上，岭南文化作为联系

behavioral patterns that Lingnan people followed long since. *Lingnan Culture: Youth Book* focuses on the six cultural forms of Lingnan culture—Lingnan painting, Cantonese music, Cantonese opera, Lingnan architecture, Lingnan customs and Cantonese delicacy, aiming to represent the artistic beauty and meaningful living style featuring Lingnan culture. The first three cultural forms have long been enjoying the nation-wide fame with their great achievements and classical works. The last three are the most direct expression of Lingnan culture, representing the everyday life of Guangzhou people, entailing such harmonious cultural concepts as inclusiveness, openness, practicality, boldness and persistence.

These cultural forms have different carriers, but they share a common cultural spirit. Lingnan painting takes Lingnan landscape and society as its artistic topics, combines Chinese and Western painting style, starting an era of "new Chinese painting". Cantonese music, with beautiful melodies, describes the everyday life of Lingnan people and their optimistic life attitudes. Cantonese opera was originally created mainly to celebrate festivals, family ceremonies, other happy occasions or to worship gods. Lingnan architecture absorbs the west architectural elements, but features Lingnan climate and geography. Lingnan customs, such as dragon boat race and other peculiar customs, represent the combination of Lingnan

纽带，更有利于促进海内外同胞大团结，大交流，大发展。

岭南文化是岭南人在与自然环境共处，适应并利用自然环境的过程中，创造出的多种物质和非物质的文化形态，承载着岭南人民在长期生活中积淀下来的价值观念、思维模式和行为方式。《岭南文化青年读本》挑选其中六种文化形态：岭南画派、广东音乐、粤剧、岭南建筑、岭南民俗和广州美食，展现岭南文化超凡的艺术创造和岭南人值得玩味的生活方式。前三者是个中翘楚。它们达到一般地方文化罕见的高度和成就，创作出许多传世不朽之作，形成具有全国性影响的流派。后三者是文化的直接表达，体现岭南人民对生活细节的要求，蕴含着开放、包容、敢为、务实、坚守等文化特质与和谐的精神理念。

虽然载体不同，但同气连枝。岭南画派以岭南风貌、时代风貌入画，折衷中西，开启包容和吸收中外绘画艺术的“新国画”时代；岁时节日、宗族祭祀、神功诞期、建醮庆典是粤剧演出最原始、最重要的场合；广东音乐多为反映岭南世俗生活和积极乐观精神的抒情优美旋律；岭南建筑既与西方建筑文化相互交流，又根据岭南特有气候、地形、地貌特点，与自然环境结合创造；岭南民俗如赛龙舟等独特的节庆民俗文化，体现岭南地域文化与海洋文化的特色融合；而了解一个地方的文化最直接的

culture with the oceanic culture. The best way to understand the culture of a place is its delicacy, and Cantonese delicacy takes one to another side of the local culture.

The six cultural forms, like six name-cards, represent the nature Guangzhou people rely on, the life Guangzhou people live and the temperament Guangzhou people feel proud of. Though they are just part of Lingnan Culture, they can also show us Lingnan Culture is always open, inclusive, creative and vigorous.

Promoting the education of Chinese excellent traditional culture, strengthening cultural self-confidence, passing traditional culture on from generation to generation, promoting its creative transformation and innovative development is a test paper handed to us by the times. By these six Lingnan name-cards, this book hopes to enter Lingnan culture and feel its tolerance, bold innovation and vitality through reading pictures and words.

途径，自然就是品味当地美食。

这六种文化形态，就像六张名片，共同体现了岭南人民自然之真，生活之真，性情之真。或许它们仅是岭南文化的一角，但也可令我们窥得岭南“不拘一格，不定一尊，不守一隅”的文化价值全貌。

加强中华优秀传统文化教育，坚定文化自信，让传统文化薪火相传，推动其创造性转化、创新性发展，是时代交给我们的一份考卷。本书希冀借这六张岭南名片，带领青年一起通过图文并茂的方式，走进岭南文化，感受它的宽厚包容、大胆创新与生机勃勃。

WORLD OF COLORS
—LINGNAN PAINTING

Lingnan painting is one important school of fine arts that rose up in South Guangdong in the early 20th century. The founders of this artistic school is Gao Jianfu, Chen Shuren and Gao Qifeng who were born in Panyu, Guangzhou, they advocated the combination of the east and the west, the old and the new to create a "new Chinese painting". Their special artistic styles won them fame in the history of modern Chinese painting. Zhao Shao'ang, Guan Shanyue, Li Xiongcai, who mainly teaching and attending activities in Guangzhou, were other masters of Lingnan painting. Lingnan painters' revolutionary spirit and their broad artistic horizon are always a treasure for the new generation of Lingnan painters.

画境

岭南画派

岭南画派是20世纪初崛起于南粤大地的重要绘画流派，开创者为生于广州番禺的高剑父、陈树人、高奇峰，提倡“折衷中西、融合古今”，探索“新国画”，以鲜明的艺术风格独步近代中国画坛。赵少昂、关山月、黎雄才等画家主要在广州教学和活动，成为影响岭南、影响中国内地乃至港澳台和海外画坛的艺术大家。岭南画派敢为人先的改革精神、雄健开阔的艺术视野，仍然哺育着新一代的岭南画人。

NEW CHINESE PAINTING

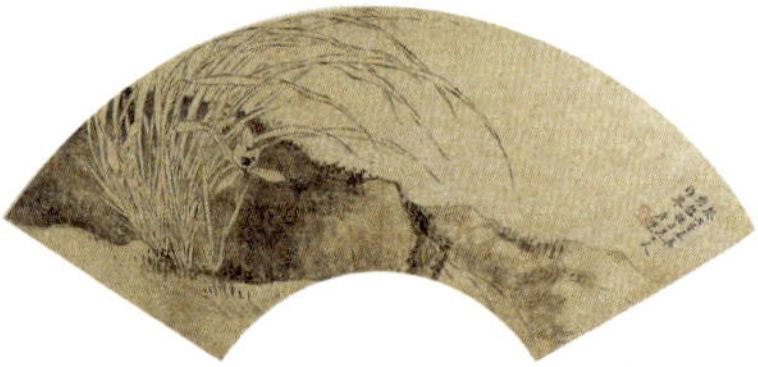

ARTISTIC REVOLUTION

In the early 20th century, Lingnan painting represented by Gao Jianfu (1879–1951), Chen Shuren (1883–1948) and Gao Qifeng (1889–1933) (the Gaos brothers and Chen) rose to fame, which initiated the revolutionary movement in Lingnan painting that lasted for about a century.

The Gaos brothers and Chen were dedicated to the reform of the old Chinese painting, advocating artistic revolution. They combined the traditional Chinese painting with the realistic techniques of the western arts, and for the first time took Lingnan landscape, social issues as their artistic subject matters, which marked the beginning of the age of "new Chinese painting".

Gao Jianfu and Chen Shuren followed Ju Chao and Ju Lian, representatives of Lingnan painting in Qing Dynasty, to learn painting, while Gao Qifeng learned from his brother Gao Jianfu. In the tide of democratic revolution and

新派国画

艺术变革

20世纪初，以“二高一陈”即高剑父（1879—1951）、陈树人（1883—1948）和高奇峰（1889—1933）为主要创始人的岭南画派在广州崛起，拉开了近百年岭南画坛大变革的序幕。

“二高一陈”致力改革旧国画，倡导“艺术革命”，将传统国画和西方写实之法相结合，开创性地以岭南风物、时代风貌入画，开启了一个属于“新国画”的时代。

高剑父和陈树人早年追随清代岭南本土画派代表人物居巢、居廉（“二居”），高剑父之弟高奇峰也是从高剑父这里间接习得“二居”画艺。在20世纪初民主革命风云和“开眼看世界”的时代风潮中，他们追随孙中山开展国民革命，加入同盟会，并游学日本，找到变革中国画的方

高剑父 Gao Jianfu

陈树人 Chen Shuren

高奇峰 Gao Qifeng

居廉 Ju Lian

居巢 Ju Chao

"opening to the world" at the beginning of the 20th century, they followed Sun Yat-sen for revolution, join Tung Meng Hui and visited Japan for inspirations of social and artistic renovation, which marked the beginning of their artistic exploration.

After he returned home in 1908 from Japan, Gao Jianfu organized his first personal exhibition to exhibit some of his experimental works. Later, Gao Jianfu and Gao Qifeng held another exhibition in Guangzhou. Their works combined the east and west artistic techniques, which proved to be completely different from the traditional Chinese painting. The peculiarities of their artistic works injected a dose of new blood into the artistic world of that time.

向，开始其艺术革新的探索。

1908年从日本回国后，高剑父在广州举办了个人的第一个画展，首次展出一批带有实验性质的作品。此后，高剑父与高奇峰再次在广州举办画展，其作品融合了中西技法，呈现出与传统国画迥然不同的面貌，鲜明新颖的独特风格让当时的画坛焕然一新。

居廉《南瓜花·螽斯》 Ju Lian · Pumpkin Flowers and Katydids

REFORM AND INNOVATION

In 1921, Gao Jianfu, Gao Qifeng and Chen Shuren exhibited their works of "new Chinese painting" in Guangzhou. They advocated reforming the traditional Chinese painting. That was the birth of the honorary title "three masters of Lingnan painting". That was the first time the masters of "new Chinese painting" showed themselves to the artistic world.

From the birth of the early "hybridity" theory to the circulation of the works of "new Chinese painting", Lingnan painters dedicated themselves to the reformation of the old tradition of Chinese painting at the turn of Qing Dynasty and the Republic of China that imitated the ancient painting in China, but their innovation came under the attack of those who tried to protect the traditional Chinese painting.

After the exhibition in Yuexiu Park in 1926, dissatisfied with the exhibition organizers' attempt to marginalized their "hybridity" painting, Gao Jianfu asked his student Fang Rending to write an article to voice their advocation to reform the traditional Chinese painting. This caused a debate between Fang Rending and Huang Bore, the representative of Chinese Painting Association. The debate lasted over two years, which was known as a controversy between the old and new schools of Chinese Paintings.

By the debate, Gao Jianfu and other masters won their fame as leading painters in Guangdong both theoretically and practically.

革旧立新

1921年，高剑父、陈树人与高奇峰创作的众多“新国画”在广州集体展出，他们同时提出革新传统国画的理论，“岭南三杰”的称号由此而来，这也是“新国画”干将们的第一次集体亮相，震动了当时的中国画坛。

从早期“折衷”理论的诞生，到“新国画”作品的传播，岭南画派一改清末民初摹古之风，遭到当时传统国画捍卫者的批评和诘难。

1926年的越秀公园游艺会后，因不满游艺会主办方将“折衷派”作品边缘化，高剑父授意学生方人定撰文，主张改革旧国画，引起论战，国画研究会则由黄般若撰文予以反击。这场笔战断断续续长达两年之久，是一场关于新旧国画的论争。

争鸣声中，高剑父等人真正在理论和实践上以“新国画”运动倡导者的形象，在广东画坛奠定了盟主的地位。

高剑父《饮马渡关图》
Gao Jianfu · Horse Drinking before Crossing the Frontier

GROWTH TO FAME

The development of Lingnan painting benefited from the contribution of Gao Jianfu, Gao Qifeng and many others. Around the 1920s, the Gaos brothers began to teach students in Guangzhou. Many Lingnan painters were their disciples.

The Chunshui Painting Academy organized by Gao Jianfu once recruited more than 100 students at its best days. Guan Shanyue, Li Xiongcai, and Fang Rending were all students of the Chunshui Painting Academy. Gao Qifeng established the Fine Arts Workshop in Guangzhou. In the last years of his life, he cultivated such famous painters as Huang Shaoqiang, Zhao Shao'ang, Ye Shaobing, and He Qiyuan in his Tianfeng Villa.

From the 1930s to the 1940s, Huang Shaoqiang, Zhao Shao'ang, Fang Rending, Guan Shanyue, Li Xiongcai, as the second generation of Lingnan painters, came to their artistic maturity. They advocated artistic revolution to save the country. They depicted the social life of Chinese people and produced many famous works, and that turned them into the leading voice of modern Chinese painting.

陈树人《长城暮鸦》
Chen Shuren · Evening Crow over the Great Wall

后学壮大

岭南画派的发展和壮大，得益于高剑父、高奇峰等人一直致力传播和继承。20世纪20年代前后，高氏兄弟先后在广州设帐授徒，培育了大批岭南画派传人。

高剑父主办的春睡画院，鼎盛时期学员超过百人，关山月、黎雄才、方人定等美术大家，都曾经是春睡画院的弟子。高奇峰在广州创办美学馆，在生命的最后几年，他还在广州天风楼培育出黄少强、赵少昂、叶少秉、何漆园等岭南名家。

20世纪三四十年代，黄少强、赵少昂、方人定、关山月、黎雄才等岭南画派二代传人的艺术风格日渐成熟，他们怀抱艺术救国的理想，深入生活，佳作频出，逐渐成长为中国近现代画坛的中坚力量。

HERITAGE AND DEVELOPMENT

Since the 1950s, Lingnan painters gradually formed their own peculiar artistic features in the mainland of China and Hong Kong.

Guan Shanyue's "Our Beautiful Motherland" (cooperated with Fu Baoshi), "Coal City", "Green Great Wall", and Li Xiongcai's "Flood Map of Wuhan", "The First Mountain of the Long March" are regarded as the representative works of realistic painting in new China. After settling in Hong Kong, Zhao Shao'ang held exhibitions in many places of the world or gave lectures, which won him a world-wide fame.

In the 1980s and the 1990s, Guan Shanyue, Li Xiongcai, Zhao Shao'ang, and Yang Shanshen, as heirs to Lingnan school of painters, remained active in the world of fine arts. Lingnan Painting Memorial was built in Guangzhou; numerous works of Lingnan painting came out; more exhibitions were held; the academic circle became more and more interested in the studies of Lingnan painting.

Guan Shanyue, Li Xiongcai and Zhao Shao'ang inherited the tradition of Lingnan painters who dedicated themselves to fine arts education while making every effort to develop the artistic tradition of Chinese painting. And their students could be seen everywhere. Today, Lingnan painting is known for its masters who were good at painting human figures, birds and flowers, landscape, and their disciples can be seen everywhere both at home and abroad.

发扬传承

从20世纪50年代开始，岭南画派的传人分别在内地和香港，发展出各具特色的艺术道路。

关山月创作出《江山如此多娇》（与傅抱石合作）、《煤都》、《绿色长城》等名作。黎雄才的《武汉防汛图卷》《长征第一山》等作品，都堪称新中国美术的现实主义扛鼎之作。赵少昂定居香港后，到世界各地举办画展、讲学，备受海内外尊崇。

20世纪八九十年代，关山月、黎雄才、赵少昂、杨善深等岭南大家以岭南画派的传人身份活跃于画坛。广州建立了岭南画派纪念馆，推动了岭南画派诸家的画集出版和展览举办工作，学界对岭南画派的研究开始勃兴。

关山月《江山如此多娇》（与傅抱石合作）
Guan Shanyue • Our Beautiful Motherland (cooperated with Fu Baoshi)

黎雄才《武汉防汛图卷》
Li Xiongcai · Flood Map of Wuhan

Lingnan painting, with Guangzhou as its birth place, has become a national and international artistic school, and provides a beautiful page in the history of Lingnan painting and Chinese painting as well.

秉承岭南画派教书育人的传统，关山月、黎雄才、赵少昂等继续弘扬中国画学传统，桃李满天下。时至今日，岭南画派在人物、花鸟、山水等各题材领域人才辈出，再传弟子遍及海内外。以广州为中心发源地的岭南画派，成为具有全国乃至世界影响的艺术流派，在百年岭南美术史乃至中国美术史上，写下绚丽璀璨的一笔。

CHANGE AND INNOVATION

COMBINATION OF THE EAST AND THE WEST

"Combination of the east and the west, the old and the new" is the ultimate pursuit of Lingnan painting.

Gao Jianfu, Chen Shuren and Gao Qifeng were known in their early years as masters of "hybridity" painting. Gao Jianfu mentioned in his articles or speeches the concept of combination of the east and the west, the old and the new to reform fine arts. He believed this to be the best art. In a word, he advocated both inheriting the tradition and absorbing the foreign elements, with an attempt to lead painting to its new form.

In their artistic practice, Lingnan painters made use of the techniques of the western painting while keeping the tradition of ink and brushes favored by traditional Chinese painting, aiming to create the modern artistic model with both the east and the west artistic elements, which gave

创新求变

折衷中西

“折衷中西，融合古今”是岭南画派最重要的精神内核。

高剑父、陈树人和高奇峰早年常以“折衷派”自称，高剑父也多次在文章和演讲中提到“折衷”，就是“要把中外古今的长处来折衷地和革新地整理一过，使之合乎中庸之道，所谓集体世界之大成”。概而言之，既要继承传统，又要借鉴外来，博采众长。

在创作实践中，岭南画派诸家在自己创作中汲取和借鉴西方绘画的技法，同时保留了传统中国画的笔墨技巧，融合出一种亦中亦西、具有现代气息的新国画范例，旨在使中国画在变革中获得新的生命力，立身于世界美术长廊。

the Chinese painting a new life and won a position in the gallery of world arts.

BOTH FORM AND CONTENT

Gao Jianfu, Gao Qifeng and Chen Shuren inherited the realistic tradition of the Jus' painting, which laid the foundation for their lifelong realistic creation. They visited Japan and there they mastered the realistic artistic techniques of Japanese and the western paintings.

In the early years when they put forward the concept of "artistic revolution", the Gaos brothers and Chen advocated realistic creation, and attacked violently the outdated imitation of the ancient painting popular at the turn of Qing Dynasty and the Republic of China. Gao Jianfu's paintings of birds, flowers and landscapes were known for their natural beauty. Chen Shuren loved painting landscapes and tried to find beauty from the nature. The eagles, dragons, tigers, fishes, pines, monkeys under Gao Qifeng's brush were all vivid and lively. Guan Shanyue, Li Xiongcai, Fang Rending, Yang Shanshen all inherited the realistic tradition of Lingnan painting and kept this tradition throughout the whole of their artistic life.

The realistic painting of Lingnan painters focused on both form and content. The eagles, lions, and tigers under the brushes of Gao Jianfu and Gao Qifeng were often symbols to show their revolutionary spirits, while the birds,

陈树人《鼎湖飞瀑》

Chen Shuren · The Falls Over Dinghu Mountain

高剑父《秋鹰》
Gao Jianfu · The Autumn Eagle

形神兼具

高剑父、陈树人、高奇峰继承了居派绘画的写实风格，奠定了其一生注重写实的创作倾向。随后，他们留学日本，也很快接受了日本和西洋的写实绘画技法。

高奇峰《猴》
Gao Qifeng • The Monkey

在提出“艺术革命”的初始阶段，“二高一陈”倡言写实，猛烈冲击了摹古之风盛行的清末民初的中国画坛。高剑父的花鸟画、山水画充满自然的生趣。陈树人最爱云游写生，寄情山水，寻找诗画创作的情趣和题材。高奇峰笔下的桀骜雄鹰、腾龙跃虎、水中群鱼、月夜松猿，都栩栩如生，富有灵性。岭南画派传人如关山月、黎雄才、方人定、杨善深等也继承了岭南画派的写生精神，并在他们一生的创作中贯穿始终。

岭南画派主张的写实，力求形神兼具。比如，高剑父、高奇峰笔下的鹰、狮子、虎等雄壮形象往往与他们抒发革命壮志的情怀联系在一起，而陈树人笔下的花鸟、山水则透露出他文人式简淡风雅的气质。

flowers, landscapes under Chen Shuren's brush expressed his pursuit for a simple life.

HIGH-BROW AND LOW-BROW

Lingnan painters advocate painting serving the society and the public by depicting both the high-brow and low-brow.

Gao Jianfu believed that "Art serves the public", Chen Shuren insisted that "Art relates to national spirit", while Gao Qifeng argued that painting "is not a dead object, but something with its own life; each age has its own peculiar spirit and experience".

As to artistic subject matters, Lingnan painting advocates depicting nothing but human figures and realistic matters, and those with epochal significance. The new cars, planes and modern buildings new to that age became the subject matters of Gao Jianfu's artistic creation. His classical works "The Fire on the East Battlefield" for the first time took war as the artistic subject. Chen Shuren's paintings depicted farmers, fishermen, cowboys, ship workers and boat trackers.

In the 1930s and the 1940s, Guan Shanyue, Li Xiongcai, Fang Rending created many artistic works depicting the battles, war victims and Japanese invaders. These paintings on common things were expressive of the war time spirit.

高剑父《东战场的烈焰》Gao Jianfu • The Fire on the East Battlefield

Lingnan painting's choice of artistic subject matters and creative techniques broadened the horizon of traditional Chinese painting, which fulfilled Lingnan painting's goal to use art to depict life, to use art to participate in social revolution, and to promote the modernization of traditional Chinese painting.

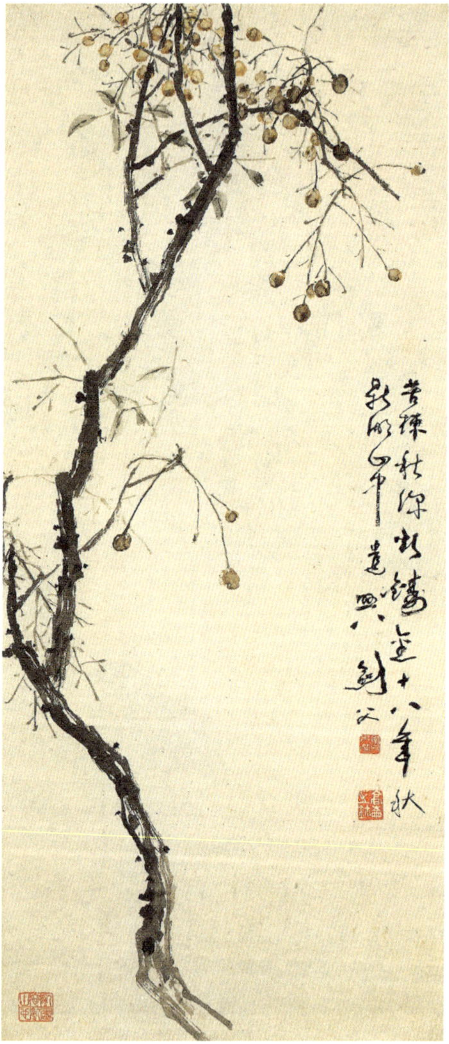

高剑父《深秋苦楝树》
Gao Jianfu • Neem in Late Autumn

雅俗共赏

岭南画派主张艺术要为时代、为民众服务，笔墨当随时代，雅俗共赏。

高剑父提出“艺术是给民众应用和欣赏的”，陈树人说“艺术关系国魂”，高奇峰也阐明“我以为画学不是一件死物，而是一件有生命，能变化的东西。每一时代自有一时代之精神和经验”。

在创作题材的选择上，岭南画派主张无人无事不可入画，尤其注重富有时代气息的事物。当时最新式的汽车、飞机以及现代建筑均被高剑父取作题材，他的经典作品《东战场的烈焰》首次将战争题材入画。陈树人也常将农夫、渔夫、牧童、船工、纤夫等劳动者入画。

20世纪三四十年代，关山月、黎雄才、方人定等创作了大量记录战地状况、民众流亡和日寇侵略暴行的作品，通俗而富于感染力，弘扬了时代抗战精神。

岭南画派对题材的拓展和画法，大大拓宽了传统中国画的视野和表现题材，实践了岭南画派以艺术介入人生、以艺术介入社会革命的主张，促进了传统国画的现代化进程。

ARTISTIC MASTERS

"THE GAOS BROTHERS AND CHEN": MASTERS

Gao Jianfu, Chen Shuren and Gao Qifeng were the founding fathers of Lingnan painting and the representatives of Lingnan painting. They were called collectively as "The Gaos Brothers and Chen", or the "three masters of Lingnan painting".

Gao Jianfu (1879-1951) was born in Panyu of Guangdong Province. He was one of the founding fathers of Lingnan painting and one of the famous fine arts educators and the leading revolutionaries of Xinhai Revolution. He learned painting skill from Ju Lian as his teacher when he was young. He was good at painting landscapes, birds, flowers, beasts and human figures, and was also good at calligraphy. In 1906, he joined Tung Meng Hui and was once appointed director of the Guangdong Branch of Tung Meng Hui. In the early years of the Republic of China, Gao Jianfu and his brother Gao Qifeng went to Shanghai

画坛大家

“二高一陈”：一代宗师

高剑父、陈树人和高奇峰是岭南画派的创始人，也是最具代表性的岭南画派人物，史称“二高一陈”，又名“岭南三杰”。

高剑父《芭蕉图》
Gao Jianfu • The Plantain

高剑父（1879—1951），广东番禺人。岭南画派创始人之一，也是辛亥革命元老和著名的美术教育家。少年时拜师居廉学画，擅画山水、花鸟、走兽、人物画，也精于书法。1906年加入同盟会，曾任同盟会广东分会会长。民国初年，与弟高奇峰赴上海创办《真相画报》。1920年被任命为广东工艺局局长兼广东甲种工业学校校长。其后辞职，逐渐淡出政坛，致力倡导“折衷中西，

高剑父《秋江独钓图》
Gao Jianfu · The Lone Fisherman on the Autumn River

and established *The True Record* there. In 1920, he was appointed director of Guangdong Bureau of Arts and Crafts as well as president of The First Industrial School of Guangdong Province. He resigned later, gradually stepping away from politics, and devoted himself to the new Chinese painting movement that combined the west and the Chinese arts as well as the old and the new artistic forms. In 1923, he established Chunshui Painting Academy in Guangzhou, and was the president of Foshan Academy of Fine Arts, professor of Sun Yat-Sen University and Nanjing Central University, cultivating lots of talents in fine arts. His masterpieces included "The Fire on the East Battle Field", "The Bleak River Mouth", "Pine, Wind and Waves in the Moonlight", "Rain" and "Bird-Tailed Dragonfly". And his collections of paintings included *Jianfu Paintings* and *Collected Paintings of Jianfu* in addition to his essay collections about fine arts *My View of Modern Chinese Paintings*. He died in Macao in 1951.

Chen Shuren (1884–1948) was born in Panyu of Guangdong Province. He learned painting from Ju Lian when he was 17 years old. He travelled to Japan twice and studied in the Japanese universities. He was also among the pioneers of Xinhai Revolution, a follower of Sun Yat-sen, the member of Tung Meng Hui. He was later officials of the government, but never gave up his artistic creation. He was a poet and a painter, good at painting landscapes and flowers, especially bombax flowers. His paintings incorporated the western painting techniques with traditional

融合古今”的新国画运动。1923年在广州创办春睡画院，并先后担任佛山美术学院院长、中山大学及南京中央大学教授等，培育了大量美术人才。代表作有《东战场的烈焰》《江关萧瑟》《松风水月图》《雨景图》《鸢尾蜻蜓》等，著有画集《剑父画谱》《剑父画集》以及画论著作《我的现代国画观》等。1951年于澳门病逝。

陈树人（1884—1948），广东番禺人。17岁开始跟从居廉学画，后两度留学日本。早年追随孙中山参加民主革命，是同盟会会员，后来历任政府要职，从政之

陈树人《岭南春色》

Chen Shuren · Spring of Lingnan Region

Chinese paintings and were characterized by their fresh simplicity. His masterpieces included "Spring of Lingnan Region", "Autumn River in the Evening Sun", "Riding the Donkey in Rain", etc.; his poems included *Early Green Grass*, *Song of Nature Beauty*, and *Collected Poems of Chunguang Villa*. As one of the founding fathers of Lingnan painting, Chen Shuren had yet his own peculiar artistic style and his own artistic ideals. He explored into the reform of traditional Chinese painting, and his exploration was integrated into a whole with his non-utilitarianist pursuit and his special understanding of poetry and painting, which helped form his vivid but detached painting style.

陈树人《五老峰冬望》
Chen Shuren • Winter View on Wulao Mount

Gao Qifeng (1889–1933), born in Panyu of Guangdong Province, the younger brother of Gao Jianfu. He was known for his paintings of beasts, flowers and birds. In his early years, he learned painting from his brother Gao Jianfu, and was indirectly a student of Ju Chao and Ju Lian. In 1907, He went to Japan together with Gao Jianfu to learn painting, and in the same year he joined Tung Meng Hui. In 1925, he was appointed the honorary professor of Lingnan University, and opened Fine Arts Workshop in Guanzhou to teach painting. In 1929, he taught painting in Tianfeng Villa. In 1933, he died of disease in Shanghai at the age of 44. His masterpieces included "The Sea Eagle", "The White Horse", "The Lion", "The Roaring Tiger", "High Mountains and Running Water" and "Lonely Monkey Calling in Snow". He published *Collections of Qifeng Paintings* and *Posthumous Paintings of Gao Qifeng*. Gao

高奇峰《双马图》
Gao Qifeng · Twin Horses

余不忘潜心画事。工诗善画，擅山水、花卉，尤以木棉花最为擅长。其绘画融会中西画法，别具淡雅清新的风格。代表画作有《岭南春色》《秋江夕照》《细雨骑驴入剑门》等，诗集有《寒绿吟草》《自然美讴歌集》《春光堂诗集》等。作为岭南画派的开创者之一，陈树人的个人创作和艺术思想自成一格。他在革新传统中国画方面也做出了独特的探索，这种探索与他超脱的个性、诗画并重的学养融为一体，最终形成立意新颖、淡雅清新的独特风格。

高奇峰（1889—1933），广东番禺人，高剑父之弟。尤擅走兽、花鸟。早年随兄高剑父学画，间接师从居巢、居廉。1907年随高剑父赴日本习画，同年加入同盟会。1925年任岭南大学名誉教授，在广州开设美学馆授徒。1929年，辟天风楼作画授徒。1933年

Qifeng was the artistic model of new Chinese painting in modern China with his peculiar pioneering paintings, known both nationally and internationally. His influences over the younger generation by his artistic education were also tremendous. His students such as Huang Shaoqiang, Zhao Shao'ang, and Ye Shaobing were all established figures in the painting circle.

关山月
Guan Shanyue

GUAN SHANYUE: PAINTERS OF LANDSCAPE

Guan Shanyue (1912–2000), originally named Guan Zepei, was born in Yangjiang of Guangdong Province. Guan Shanyuan was one of the four masters of Lingnan painting that included also Zhao Shao'ang, Li Xiongcai, and Yang Shanshen. He was also a fine arts educator. He was good at painting landscapes, human figures, flowers and birds, and was especially known for his landscape paintings and paintings of plum blossoms.

Guan Shanyue's paintings all over his life were always an echo to the times he lived in. He observed the revolutionary principle of Lingnan painting that art served the public. He combined his artistic creation with the social customs and the temporal spirit. Over half a century's artistic career, he created many works with peculiar styles that reflected the temporal spirit of his age, so he occupied a very important position in the history of Chinese fine arts. His artistic works helped elevate Lingnan painting that

在上海病逝，年仅44岁。代表作品有《海鹰》《白马》《雄狮》《虎啸》《山高水长》《孤猿啼雪》等。出版有《奇峰画集》《高奇峰先生遗画集》等。高奇峰以富有开拓性又独具个人风格的绘画，成为近代画坛革新中国画的艺术典范，以卓越的艺术成就享誉海内外画坛，并通过美术教育影响了一代岭南画人，他的弟子黄少强、赵少昂、叶少秉等都在画坛卓有建树。

关山月：从头画江山

关山月（1912—2000），原名关泽霈，广东阳江人。与赵少昂、黎雄才、杨善深并称为当代岭南画派四大家，他同时也是美术教育家。擅长山水、人物、花鸟，尤以山水和写梅著称。

关山月一生的创作都与时代共振。他秉承岭南画派所倡导的

关山月《长城内外尽朝晖》
Guan Shanyue • Morning Sunlight over the Great Wall

关山月《榕荫曲》
Guan Shanyue • Song of Banyan Shade

depicted the epochal spirit to a new height either in terms of aesthetic beauty or in terms of artistic achievement, and became the model of the everlastingly innovative Chinese fine arts.

He cooperated with Fu Baoshi to create the large painting "Our Beautiful Motherland" that was hung in the

关山月《新开的公路》 Guan Shanyue • New Highway

关山月《俏不争春》
Guan Shanyue • Serene Spring Beauty

Great Hall of the People in Beijing, one of the most well-known paintings in the history of new Chinese fine arts. Other well-known paintings include "The Light Boat Passing through the Mountains" hung in Ziguang Hall of the State Council of the People's Republic of China, "Spring is Coming" in China Hall of the United Nations, "Song of Plum Blossoms" in the Great Hall of the People, and "Song of Huanghe River" in the hall of Chinese People's Political Consultative Conference. He also published *Collections of Guan Shanyue's Paintings*, *Selected Paintings of Guan Shanyue*, *Love of My Hometown*, and *Song of My Motherland*.

"艺术要民众化"等革新主张，将自己的创作和社会风貌、时代精神紧密融为一体，在其半个多世纪的艺术生涯中，创作出大量紧扣时代脉搏、独具个人风格的传世之作，在新中国美术发展史中占有重要地位，这些作品无论在审美意识还是在艺术成就上，都将岭南画派表现时代精神的理念上升到一个新的高度，成为中国画艺术不断求新求变的典范。

关山月曾与傅抱石共同为北京人民大会堂创作巨幅国画《江山如此多娇》，是新中国美术史上最广为人知的作品之一；为国务院紫光阁作《轻舟已过万重山》；为联合国中国厅作《报春图》；为北京人民大会堂创作《国香赞》；为全国政协礼堂作《黄河颂》。有《关山月画集》《关山月作品选集》《乡土情》《山河颂》等出版。

关山月《绿色长城》
Guan Shanyue • The Green Great Wall

ZHAO SHAO'ANG: I AM THE VOICE

赵少昂
Zhao Shao'ang

Zhao Shao'ang (1905–1998) was born in Guangzhou while his family were from Panyu of Guandong, and later he moved to Hong Kong. At 16, he entered Gao Qifeng's Fine Arts Workshop to learn painting, and was one of the "Seven of Tianfeng". He was good at painting flowers, birds, insects, fishes and other animals, especially good at flower-bird painting. His masterpieces included "White Peacock", "Tung-Flower Green Peacock", "Serenity", "Daffodils", "Tiger in the Grass" and "Kingfisher". His books included *Collections of Shao'ang's Paintings*, *Recent Paintings of Zhao Shao'ang*, *Collections of Zhao Shao'ang's Paintings*, *Rongbaozhai Paintings 15: Flowers, Birds, Grass and Insects—Zhao Shao'ang*, and *Practical Science of Painting*.

Zhao Shao'ang began to be very active in the painting circle since the 1920s. He frequently attended exhibitions and published many collections of his paintings. At 25, his "White Peacock" won the gold medal at Belgium World's Fair, which won him an international fame. In the same year, Zhao Shao'ang and Huang Shaoqiang together established Lingnan Art Institute in Guangzhou that had great influences over modern Lingnan fine arts education in modern China. In 1948, Zhao Shao'ang moved to Hong Kong where he reopened Lingnan Art Institute to teach painting. Later, he devoted himself to fine arts education and artistic creation and travelled to many countries for his

赵少昂：自有我在

赵少昂（1905—1998），广东番禺人，生于广州，后移居香港。16岁时进入岭南画派创始人高奇峰的美学馆学画，是高奇峰门下著名的“天风七子”之一。他擅长花鸟、虫鱼和动物，尤以花鸟画扬名国际。代表作品有《白孔雀》《桐花孔翠》《悠然自得》《自葆冰心不着尘》《自有雄风藏草泽》《晚翠》等，有《少昂画集》《赵少昂近作集》《赵少昂画集》《荣宝斋画谱(十五)•花鸟草虫部分•赵少昂》《实用绘画学》等画册及专集出版。

赵少昂《枇杷图》 Zhao Shao'ang • Loquat

赵少昂《白孔雀》 Zhao Shao'ang • White Peacock

artistic career.

In the 1950s and 1960s, Zhao Shao'ang travelled to many countries. He held painting exhibitions there and gave lectures, aiming to tell stories of Chinese arts. Wherever

赵少昂从20世纪20年代开始活跃于画坛，广泛参与书画展览，有众多画集出版。25岁时，他的《白孔雀》在比利时万国博览会展出并获金奖，声名鹊起，同年他与同门黄少强在广州创办在近代岭南美术教育史上影响巨大的“岭南画苑”。1948年，赵少昂移居香港后，重开“岭南艺苑”授徒，此后他从事艺术教育和绘画创作，并游历海外。

20世纪50至60年代，赵少昂漫游世界多个国家，举办画展和讲学，致力宣扬中国艺术，所到之处都备受好评，真正做到了雅俗共赏，中外共鸣，为弘扬和传播岭南画派做出了杰出贡献。

赵少昂《群鸟话夕阳》 Zhao Shao'ang • Birds Talk in Sunset

he went, he was warmly welcomed and praised by the audience, either high-brow or low-brow, at home or abroad, which promoted the development of Lingnan painting.

LI XIONGCAI: INGENIOUS MASTER OF BRUSH AND INK

黎雄才
Li Xiongcai

Li Xiongcai (1910–2001), born in Zhaoqing of Guangdong Province, was a leading representative of Lingnan Painting and a fine arts educator. In his early years, he learned painting from Gao Jianfu as a student of Chunshui Painting Academy. Later he visited Japan to study arts, and was once appointed the counselor and professor of Guangzhou Academy of Fine Arts.

Li Xiongcai was good at painting landscapes, flowers, birds, human figures, especially good at paintings landscape. His landscape paintings featured especially pine trees, rocks and water, and were known for his hazy green mountains

黎雄才《井冈山朱砂冲哨口》
Li Xiongcai · Sentry Box at Zhushachong of Jinggang Mountain

黎雄才：笔精墨妙

黎雄才（1910—2001），广东肇庆人。岭南画派的杰出代表和美术教育家，早年师从高剑父，为春睡画院弟子，后留学日本，曾任广州美术学院顾问、教授。

黎雄才擅长山水、花鸟、人物，尤精山水画。他的山水画中，松、石、水别有特色，以重笔浓墨的青绿山水闻名，画作气势浑厚，老辣雄劲，尤以“笔精”与“墨妙”达到形神兼备，自具风貌，被画界誉为“黎家山水”。

其画松尤为一绝，以焦墨绘针叶，给人刚劲繁茂之感，被称为“黎家松”。代表作有《潇湘夜雨图》《武汉防汛图卷》《鼎湖飞瀑》《松风水月》《森林》《三峡》《迎客松》等，出版有《黎雄才山水画谱》《黎雄才画选》《黎雄才画集》《黎雄才作品欣赏》等画集。

黎雄才《黄花岗夕照》
Li Xiongcai · Evening Glow in Yellow Granite

painted with heavy ink. His paintings were always vigorous, powerful, featuring complicated strokes and exquisite use of the ink, and thus were often termed as "Li's Landscape."

His paintings of pine trees were especially famous, featuring clear-cut leaves in black ink and great vitality, and thus were often called "Li's Pine Trees". His masterpieces included "Rain over Xiangjiang River", "Flood Map of Wuhan", "The Falls over Dinghu Moutain", "Pine, Wind and Waves in the Moonlight", "Forests", "Three Gorges", and "Welcoming Pine Tree"; his books included *Landscape Paintings of Li XiongCai*, *Selection of Li Xiongcai's Paintings*, *Collections of Li Xiongcai's Paintings*, and *Appreciation of Li Xiongcai's Paintings*.

Li Xiongcai inherited the realistic tradition of Lingnan painting. He tried to reform the traditional artistic creation mode of Chinese painting to depict the social life and the natural glamor of his age with his brush and ink. His large-size painting "Flood Map of Wuhan" won the attention of the whole painting circle. Because of the new model used here to paint the landscape, this painting was acclaimed by the circle of fine arts as "Flood-Fighting Epic". In June 2001, Li Xiongcai won the first Chinese Fine Arts Achievement Award issued by China Federation of Literary and Art Circles and China Artists Association. In December 2001, he died at Guangzhou at the age of 91.

Adviser of this Chapter: Wang Jian (Director and deputy research librarian of Education Committee of Guangzhou Art Museum)

黎雄才《森林》
Li Xiongcai · Forests

承继岭南画派的现实精神，黎雄才努力突破传统程式，建构起与新时代、新生活相连的笔墨语言，为中国画表现时代生活和山河新貌做出了成功的探索。其巨幅长卷《武汉防汛图卷》一问世即备受瞩目，因其创造了一种新的山水画表现范式，被美术界誉为“防汛史诗”。2001年6月，黎雄才荣获由中国文学艺术界联合会、中国美术家协会颁发的第一届“中国美术金彩奖成就奖”。同年12月，他在广州病逝，终年91岁。

本章顾问：王　坚（广州艺术博物院宣教工作委员会主任、副研究馆员）

WORLD OF SOUND —CANTONESE MUSIC

Cantonese music is a kind of folk music produced on traditional stringed and woodwind intruments strings that are popular in Guangzhou. It is commonly believed that it is a combination of local music (such as Muyu opera, Dragon Boat opera, Nanyin opera, and Cantonese songs, eight-sound orchestra, drum-gong troupe) with those ancient Central China music, melodies of Kun opera, South China melodies, religious music, and western music that were brought to Pearl River Delta. After years and years of merging and adaptations, it broke free from the accompaniment music of operas and developed into an independent pure musical form different from other traditional Chinese music.

The Hes, the founder of Cantonese music, were born in Shawan Village of Panyu in Guangzhou. They greatly contributed to Cantonese musical creation, performance and education.

聆音

广东音乐

广东音乐，是流传于广东的民间丝竹音乐。一般观点认为，它是本地民间艺术（木鱼、龙舟、南音、粤讴、八音班、锣鼓柜）与历代流传到珠江三角洲的中原古乐、昆曲牌子、江南小调、宗教音乐、西方音乐等相结合，经过长时间孕育孵化，从戏曲音乐伴奏中独立出来，形成的纯器乐化的中国传统民间器乐种类。

广东音乐的开山人物“何氏三杰”均生于广州番禺沙湾古镇，在广东音乐的创作、演奏、教学上取得杰出成就。

CADENCE OF STRINGS

ROOT IN FOLK CULTURE

Pearl River Delta featured a mild climate, crisscrossing rivers, colorful produces and prosperous economy, which necessitated the local people's desire for rich cultural life and led to the birth of the diversified cultural forms. It was believed that "Guangdong people love singing, so whenever there are ceremonies, they sing songs for celebration". Many local opera melodies like Muyu opera, Dragon Boat opera, Nanyin opera, and Cantonese songs and opera troupes were very popular in Guangdong at the turn of Qing Dynasty and the Republic of China. There were also eight-sound orchestra that sang local Cantonese opera, Cantonese songs and drum-gong troupe that played pure music, which were combined later into one group called "Eight-Sound Drum-Gong Orchestra".

The Hes family at North Village of Shawan in Panyu of Guangdong that was often called "the hometown of

粤韵
飞扬

根植民间

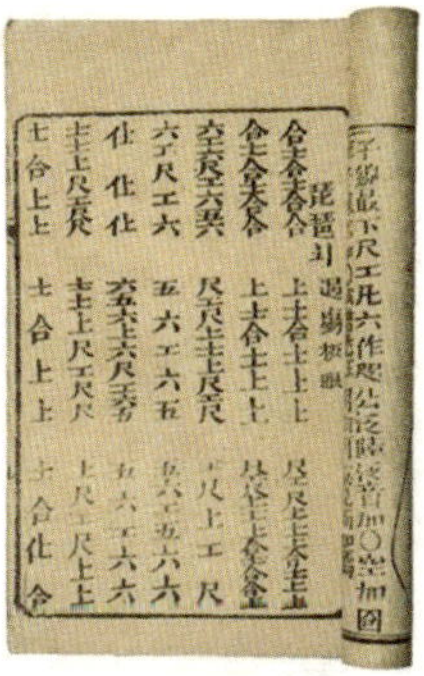

《粤讴》内容
Content of Cantonese love songs

珠江三角洲气候温和，河涌交错，物产丰富，经济繁荣使当地人民对文化生活产生迫切需求，民间艺术丰富多彩。“粤俗好歌，凡有吉庆，必唱歌以为欢乐。”民间流行木鱼、龙舟、南音、粤讴、粤曲等多种地方曲艺曲种，清末民初盛行的民间社团，有演唱本地粤剧、粤曲的八音班，及纯粹以乐器吹奏粤剧曲牌为主的锣鼓柜，二者后来合为一体，称“八音锣鼓柜”。

清代广东音乐发源地番禺沙湾北村何氏家族的何博众是“广东音乐奠基人”。他深受祖辈礼乐传家的影响，不仅琵琶技艺精湛，独创“十指琵琶法”享誉全国。还对北方乐曲和本地流行的粤讴、南音等

Cantonese music" included one guy named He Bozhong, the "founder of Cantonese music". Influenced by his family who were good at music, he was good at pipa playing, creating the well-known "ten-finger pipa playing technique". He was also familiar with the northern music and popular local Cantonese songs and Nanyin opera. Based on the ancient folk music and foreign music he collected and adapted, as well as on his personal experience, he created such musical works as "Plantains in the Rain", "The Dragon Boat Race Champion", "Starving Horse Shaking the Bells" and "Startled Birds". Influenced by He Bozhong, there were over a hundred people in the Hes family who dedicated themselves to musical or opera performances.

PROCESSING AND IMPROVEMENT

丘鹤俦
Qiu Hechou

The early Cantonese music was created by the musicians orally and tried on musical instruments based on their oral description. The learners needed careful observation and memorization. Qiu Hechou (1880–1942), born in Taishan, the initiator and developer of Cantonese music and the educator in Cantonese music, collected and processed the folk music and ancient music, folk melodies, Cantonese songs, Cantonese opera in Guangdong Province that were popular in the 1920s, and produced his book *Introduction to Stringed Music* in 1917 which was the first textbook that helped reading musical scores.

熟悉于心，在收集、整理、改编民间音乐、古曲、外来乐曲基础上，结合生活体验，创作《雨打芭蕉》《赛龙夺锦》《饿马摇铃》《鸟惊喧》等广东音乐初稿。受何博众影响，何氏家族从事广东音乐及粤剧表演的多达百人。

启蒙发展

初期广东音乐是创作者心里自编成谱，手弹口授，学者则是仔细观摩，耳听心记。“广东音乐的启蒙者和发展者”，从事广东音乐教学的台山人丘鹤俦（1880—1942）对20世纪20年代前后流行的广东民间音乐、广东流行古调、民间乐曲、粤曲、粤剧等做收集整理工作，1917年出版《弦歌必读》，教人记谱，该书是广东音乐最早的教本。

清代的一支广东乐队

A Cantonese music band in the Qing Dynasty

20世纪三四十年代的“私伙局”
Amateur musical bands in the 1930s and the 1940s

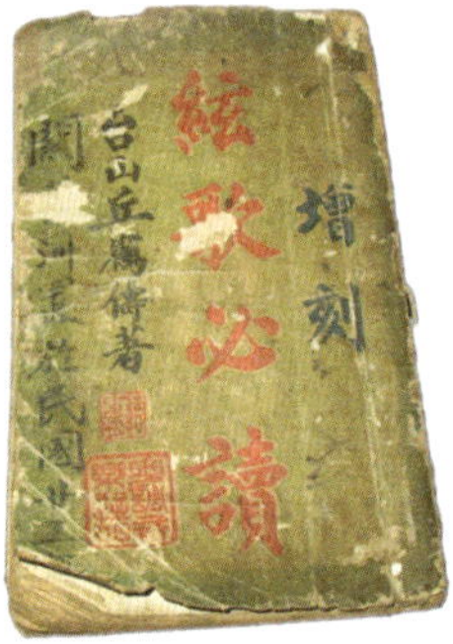

《弦歌必读》
Introduction to Stringed Music

In the early years of the Republic of China, many intellectuals often gathered to play Cantonese musical works in unprofessional musical bands. In such organizations as “the Hall” or “Cuilin” in Shawan of Panyu, the musical masters like the “three Hes”, famous opera performer and singer Chen Jian, musical masters Lü Wencheng, Yin Zizhong, He Dasha, and the “Nanhai Thirteenth Son” worked together to discuss musical creation. Based on the discussion, He Liutang provided the musical scores for He Bozhong’s “The Dragon Boat Race Champion”, “Plantains in the Rain” and “Starving Horse Shaking the Bells”, which became the masterpiece of Cantonese music.

GOLDEN AGE

The years between the 1920s and the 1930s were the golden age of Cantonese music.

街头的“私伙局”
Amateur musical bands in the street

夜晚的“私伙局”
Amateur musical bands at night

民国初期，文人结社演奏广东音乐曲艺的“私伙局”风气盛行，著名的有番禺沙湾“大厅”“翠林”等社团。广东音乐大师“何氏三杰”与曲艺名伶、演唱艺人陈鉴，音乐界大师吕文成、尹自重、何大傻以及粤剧编剧南海十三郎等交往频繁，相互切磋。在此基础上，何柳堂用记谱的形式，整理、改编祖父何博众传下的《赛龙夺锦》《雨打芭蕉》《饿马摇铃》等乐曲，使它们成为广东音乐不朽之作。

黄金时代

20世纪20至30年代，是广东音乐的黄金时代。

民间乐社遍布粤、港、澳三地，并向北及海外粤籍华人居住地扩散。国内各大城市，甚至延安，都能听到广东音乐的演奏。

工业文明繁荣推动广东音乐迅速发展。唱片业兴起成为普及广东音乐的重要契机。当时香港、上海各大唱片公司录制的唱片中，

Folk musical organizations could be seen everywhere in Guangzhou, Hong Kong and Macao, and were also common in the overseas Chinese communities. In many big cities, including Yan'an, Cantonese music could be heard.

The industrial prosperity promoted the rapid development of Cantonese music. The appearance of records provided an important channel for the publication of Cantonese music. Among all the records produced by the record companies in Hong Kong and Shanghai, 526 of them were of Cantonese music. The radio station and silent films in the early years of new China used a lot of Cantonese musical works and Cantonese opera music. Cantonese music was also played in train stations, docks, train coaches or on ships. And there appeared professional musical bands and musical players. A big number of musical scores for Cantonese music were printed in this period which promoted the publication of Cantonese music.

This was also the years when Cantonese opera developed quickly. Cantonese music and Cantonese opera together attracted the musicians of Cantonese music for the reformation in Cantonese opera. Among them, He Yunian did the biggest contribution to the reform in Cantonese opera accompaniment music and the singing styles of Cantonese opera. Cantonese opera and Cantonese songs used directly Cantonese music for their creation, and many of the musical pieces became quite well-known.

20世纪30至40年代，广东新月唱片公司发行的广东音乐唱片

Cantonese music records released by Guangdong New Moon Records Company from the 1930s to 1940s

上海百代唱片封面
Cover of Shanghai EMI Record

广东音乐多达526首。中国早期电台和无声电影都大量使用广东音乐和粤曲，车站、码头、火车、轮船上盛行播放广东音乐，出现了专职乐队和乐手。广东音乐琴谱曲集在这个阶段大量印制，也对普及推广大有裨益。

这个时期也是粤剧繁荣发展的时期，广东音乐与粤剧相互促进，许多广东音乐家参与粤剧改革，其中何与年对粤剧伴奏和唱腔设计贡献最大。粤剧、粤曲直接使用广东音乐填词，许多成为家喻户晓的金曲。

乐器革新

早期广东音乐乐队是“五架头”组合，包含二弦、竹提胡、三弦、月琴和笛五种主要乐器。主奏乐器二弦弓硬弦粗，音乐风格粗

INSTRUMENT IMPROVEMENT

The early Cantonese musical bands used "five-piece" combinations, including mainly two-stringed musical instruments, bamboo erhu, three-stringed musical instruments, yueqin and flutes. The leading musical instrument was the two-stringed musical instruments with hard bows and thick strings. The music produced on such instruments was vigorous and high-pitched. And this combination of musical instruments was called the "hard-bow combination".

In 1926, the famous er'hu player Lü Wencheng and the violinist Situ Mengyan cooperated and replaced the silk string for the outer string of erhu with the steel string used on the violin, and the result was Gaohu. Gaohu was known for its sonorous sound, rich tonality and strong expressive power, and soon became the major musical instruments. The five pieces composed of Gaohu, qinqin, dulcimer, holed bamboo flute, and coconut-boxed erhu were called the "soft-bow combination".

In the 1930s, the other western musical instruments such as violin, saxophone, guitar, woodwind, jazz drum became the fashion and were introduced into the musical bands. He Dasha, for example, changed the western guitar into the three-stringed guitar proper for Cantonese music; Yin Zizhong reset the tonality of the strings of the violin to make it produce sound that fitted Cantonese music. All these made Cantonese music sound more colorful.

犷，音色高亢嘹亮，因此被称为“硬弓组合”。

1926年著名二胡演奏家吕文成和小提琴制作家司徒梦岩共同研究，将二胡外弦由丝弦改为小提琴用的钢丝弦，创制出高胡。高胡音域扩大，音色更丰富，表现力大大加强，成为新的主奏乐器。由高胡、秦琴、扬琴、洞箫、椰胡组成的五架头，被称为“软弓组合”。

20世纪30年代其他西洋乐器如小提琴、萨克斯管、吉他、木管、爵士鼓等作为一种时髦，也被引入乐队演奏。何大傻把西洋吉他改制成广东音乐三线吉他；尹自重重新给小提琴定弦，使其音色与广东音乐韵味相称，也为广东音乐增色不少。

广东音乐的器乐演奏 Instrument performance of Cantonese music

Cantonese music proved to be very influential and was borrowed by many other artistic forms. Cantonese music composer Xian Xinghai was a native of Panyu. The "Dragon Boat Dance", the first segment of his 1935 symphony *National Liberation*, was taken from the Cantonese music "The Dragon Boat Race Champion". The composer of *Dagger Society Suite*, the folk dance created in Shanghai in the 1960s, mentioned that "The Dragon Boat Race Champion" provided inspiration for his creation of the thematic music for the dance.

Cantonese Music Creation Contest was first launched in 1995; by 2017 six contests were held, and there occurred many excellent Cantonese musical works. These musical works kept the traditional playing techniques of Cantonese music while making innovation in musical structures and layout of the sounds.

广东音乐进入国家级非物质文化遗产名录
Cantonese music has been on the list of intangible culutral heritages

广东音乐1997年新春音乐会
New Year Concert of Cantonese Music in 1997

泽被后世

广东音乐影响深远，为其他艺术所借鉴。粤籍作曲家冼星海是番禺人，1935年创作的交响乐章《民族解放交响乐》第一段《龙船舞》，即取材于《赛龙夺锦》。20世纪60年代上海创作的民族舞蹈《小刀会》，主创者也提及《赛龙夺锦》是他主题音乐的创作灵感。

1995年，广东创办广东音乐创作大赛，至2017年举办了六届，大批优秀的广东音乐新作不断涌现。这些作品既保留了广东音乐的传统旋法特点，在曲式结构及和声的布局上又独具新意。

GLAMOR OF CANTONESE MUSIC

SIMPLISTIC CLASSICAL BEAUTY

The Hes, the founders of Cantonese music, were born in a scholarly family. As the leisure class, they created music as an important interest. So the music they created mainly depicted the leisurely life the rich people and the natural beauty for the lyrical effects, and a few sang about the times they lived in. All in all, these musical works were free, lively, melodious, and intoxicating with beautiful melodies. The three Hes, with their musical works, were often classified as the "elegant school".

The creators of Cantonese music took inspiration from their life experiences and the folk customs. Their musical works such as "Xihu Lake of Mid-Autumn" and "Three Pools Mirroring the Moon" were lyrical by describing the natural scenes, while "The Lions Playing with the Silk Ball" and "The Dragon Boat Race Champion" described the folk customs. Art was derived from life, which provided

粤乐风采

幽雅古朴

广东音乐的开拓者何氏家族经济雄厚，出身书香门第，音乐是他们生活中重要的兴趣爱好。因此音乐作品的内容多为吟风赏月、自然景观描写、个人情怀抒发，反映时代特点的作品不多。故而音

沙湾广东音乐馆 Cantonese Music Museum at Shawan

Cantonese musical works with special freshness, vigor and simplicity.

SKETCH OF THE AGE

Growing over the times, Cantonese musical creation was influenced greatly by the social trends and the foreign music at that time. He Yunian borrowed a lot from the western music and created such musical pieces

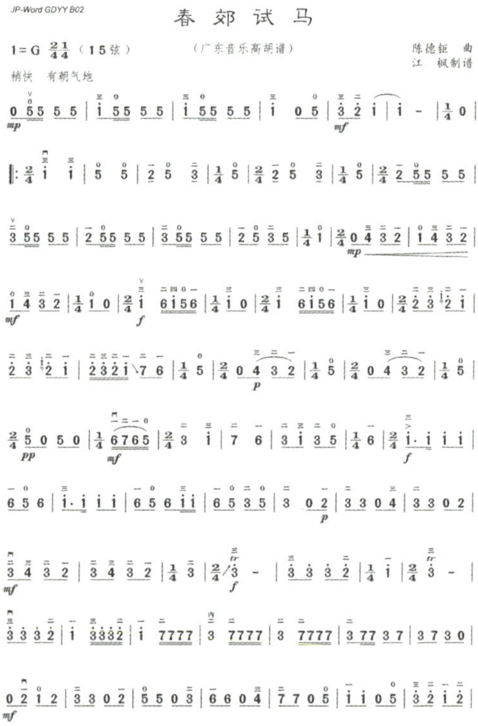

《春郊试马》高胡谱
Musical score for "Horse-Riding in the Spring Suburb" by Gaohu

春郊试马

扫描二维码
感受广东音乐

舞剧《沙湾往事》之《雨打芭蕉》
"Plantains in the Rain" in the Dance Drama *The Past of Shawan*

乐风格轻松活泼、抒情优美，旋律细腻柔美，令人陶醉，何氏三杰也被称为“典雅派”。

创作者既从生活体验出发，也受民间风俗影响。从创作曲目看，既有《平湖秋月》《三潭映月》等描绘自然风景、借景抒情的，也有如《狮子滚球》《赛龙夺锦》等描写民间习俗的。艺术源于生活，广东音乐作品始终带着清新、刚劲、古朴的生活气息。

时代剪影

随着时代变迁，广东音乐的创作也受到当时思潮和外来音乐的影响。何与年借鉴西方音乐创作的《广州青年》《蝶浪》，表达抗日救亡的《骇浪》。何少霞受民主主义进步思想影响，创造积极向

as "Guangzhou Youth", "Waving Butterflies" and "Big Waves" that sang about the anti-Japanese patriotism of Chinese people. Inspired by the revolutionary ideas of the democratic movement, He Shaoxia created such optimistic musical works as "Willows in the Fields" and "The General Trying His Horse". "The Milky Way Meet" took inspirations from the historical past to echo the present society. In the late 1930s, Lü Wencheng created "Victory" and "Waking Lions" to depict the national pride of Chinese people to fight against the Japanese invaders.

INCORPORATION OF THE WEST ART

The Japanese invasion brought forth broken families and loss of millions of lives. To live on, Cantonese musicians tried instrumental ensemble to play "spirit music" to echo the trend of popular music and the western music played in the entertainment places. All the players used the western musical instruments (sometimes including some Chinese musical instruments), which produced strongly rhythmic music and featured exaggerated performances. The scholars had different opinions about this musical form, but it was an expression of the open characteristics of Cantonese music.

上题材的作品《陌头柳色》《将军试马》。《银河会》等作品取材历史、借古讽今。20世纪30年代后期更有吕文成创作的表达抗日救亡、民族斗争精神的《凯旋》《醒狮》等名曲。

洋为中用

抗战爆发，山河破碎，人如蝼蚁。为了生存，广东音乐艺人顺应当时歌舞厅流行音乐和西方音乐的风格，运用“精神音乐”的合奏形式，演奏者全部采用西洋乐器（或也吸收一些中国乐器）表演，节奏强烈，动作夸张。尽管研究者对这种音乐形式各执一词，但也体现了广东音乐“不拘一格、灵活善变”的特点。

小提琴 Violin

MASTERS OF CANTONESE MUSIC

THREE MASTERS FROM HE FAMILY

独具岭南特色的广东沙湾古镇
Shawan Ancient Town, Guangdong Province with Lingnan characteristics

Three persons from the Hes in Shawan Village of Panyu in Guangdong Province, namely He Liutang, He Yunian and He Shaoxia, were often called the "Three Masters from He Family" for their great contribution to Cantonese musical creation, performance and education.

音乐巨匠

何氏三杰

番禺区沙湾古镇何氏家族的何柳堂、何与年、何少霞三人，因其在广东音乐创作、演奏、教学上的杰出成就，被尊称为广东音乐“何氏三杰”。

三稔厅 Sanren Hall

He Liutang: A Transitional Figure

He Liutang (1874–1933), who was born in Shawan of Panyu in Guangdong, was the grandson of the famous pipa player and musical composer He Bozhong. He was a transitional figure in the history of Cantonese music. He made four adaptations to He Bozhong's "Ships Crowding Onward", changed this musical work played on stringed musical instruments to one ensemble of wind and percussion instruments, and finally produced his masterpiece "The Dragon Boat Race Champion" that proved to be a perfect integration of content and form. His musical works included "Seven Stars with the Moon", "The Embroidered Love Letter", "The Drunkard Catching the Moon", "The Girl's Love", "Farewell in the Poplars" and "Startled Birds", which were characterized by their diverse changes of tone colors and rich images. This was his greatest contribution to Cantonese music.

He Yunian: A Prolific Composer

He Yunian (1880–1962), who was born in Shawan of Panyu in Guangdong, and He Liutang were cousins. He learned pipa playing from He Liutang since his childhood. He was also an excellent player of the three-stringed instruments, dulcimer and many other musical instruments. He was also a prolific composer of Cantonese music. His musical works consisted of more than 30 musical pieces, including such classical works as "Moon in the Cool Pond", "Flower Appreciating on the Walking Horse" and "Crying Bird in the Yard". He Yunian

何柳堂：承上启下

何柳堂 He Liutang

何柳堂（1874—1933），广东番禺沙湾镇人，是琵琶演奏家、作曲家何博众的孙子，在广东音乐发展史上起到了承上启下的作用。他将何博众的《群舟攘渡》进行修改，四易其稿，从原来的丝竹音乐改编为吹打乐合奏形式，创作了思想性与艺术性完美结合的上乘之作《赛龙夺锦》。他创作了《七星伴月》《回文锦》《金仇捞月》《玉女思春》《垂杨三复》《鸟惊喧》等名曲，采用跳跃节奏、顿音及唢呐乐器等，使得音乐调色变化极多，形象丰富，对广东音乐作出了重大贡献。

何与年：多产作家

何与年 He Yunian

何与年（1880—1962），广东番禺沙湾镇人，与何柳堂为堂兄弟，自幼随何柳堂学琵琶，后又精通三弦、扬琴等乐器，是广东音乐的多产作家，留于后世的广东音乐有《寒潭印月》《走马看花》《上苑啼莺》等作品30余首，作品注重内心感情的抒发，风格狂放。他还根据粤剧剧情增加过场音乐，解决了粤剧场次衔接过程中的静场问题。这类过场音乐经后来的不断发展成为独立名曲，奠定了广东音乐在粤剧中的地位。

stressed the flow of emotion and his musical works were often lyric and energetic. He also adapted the interlude music for Cantonese opera to solve the problem of temporary silence on the stage. After years of development, the interlude became an independent kind of music, which determined the position of Cantonese music in Cantonese opera.

He Shaoxia: A Master of Musical Instruments

He Shaoxia (1894–1942), who was born in Shawan of Panyu in Guangdong, grew up in an intellectual family. He received very good education and was good at playing the pipa, three-stringed instruments and many other musical instruments. He was nicknamed "Pipa Devil" for his excellent performance on pipa. He finished his middle school education in Guangzhou. After graduation, he returned to Shawan and taught music in a primary school there. In his spare time, he studied music together with his uncle He Liutang and He Yunian. The various decorative sounds in the third draft of "The Dragon Boat Race Champion" were his contribution. He Shaoxia was a good musical composer, and he was especially good at composing musical pieces for women performers. The classical pieces sung by the famous woman singer Zhang Yue'er in the 1920s, namely "Melancholy Traveler in Autumn" and "The Craftsmen", were his creation. His masterpieces included "Lü Gong Playing with the Water", "The Town-Fellows", "Leifeng Tower in the Sunset" and "Spring Bees and Butterflies".

何少霞 He Shaoxia

何少霞：乐器高手

何少霞（1894—1942），广东番禺沙湾镇人，出身书香世家，受过良好教育，精通琵琶、三弦及各种乐器，被称为“琵琶精”。他在广州读中学，毕业后回沙湾担任小学音乐老师，教学之余，与远房叔父何柳堂、何与年研究广东音乐，《赛龙夺锦》第三稿中很多花音，就是他经手整理的。何少霞善于创作乐曲及为女伶撰曲，20世纪20年代著名的歌伶张月儿名曲《游子悲秋》《一代艺人》就是他创作的。其代表作还有《吕宫戏水》《下里巴人》《雷峰夕照》《蜂蝶争春》等。

何少霞故居
Former residence of He Shaoxia

Lü Wencheng: A Master of Cantonese Music

吕文成 Lü Wencheng

Lü Wencheng (1898–1981), born in Zhongshan county, was a famous composer and player of Cantonese music. He was the representative of Cantonese music in its prime stage and was often called the master of Cantonese music. He was a player, composer, reformer and educator in one. He invented, through adaptation, the most important musical instrument of Cantonese music—gaohu, a C-keyed erhu. Lü Wencheng was the most prolific composer of Cantonese music. He created "Xihu Lake of Mid-Autumn", "Fisherman's Song in the Evening" and "Step on Step". He was also good at playing the Cantonese erhu, dulcimer, xylophone, violin and many other instruments. And he was often called "Dr. Erhu".

Yin Zizhong: King of Violin

Yin Zizhong (1903–1985), was a famous violinist and composer in Cantonese music. His family came from Dongguan of Guangdong Province, but he was born in Shunde, and later he moved to Hong Kong. Yin Zizhong was known all over China as a "Cantonese violinist", often nicknamed as the "king of violin". Yin Zizhong was the forerunner to nationalize the violin. In the 1930s, he was the first musician who introduced the violin into Cantonese music and the accompaniment music of Cantonese opera. Based on the techniques of playing the stringed musical instruments in Guangdong Province and the basic playing techniques of the violin, he created a set of playing

四大天王

吕文成：粤乐宗师

吕文成（1898—1981），广东著名音乐演奏家、作曲家，中山县人，广东音乐成熟时期的代表人物，被称为“粤乐一代宗师”。他是集演奏、创作、乐队改革、高质量教学于一身的大家，改制创造出广东音乐最重要的代表乐器高胡。吕文成是创作乐曲最多的音乐名家，他创作改编的作品有《平湖秋月》《渔歌唱晚》《步步高》等名曲。他还擅长粤胡、扬琴、木琴、小提琴等乐器演奏，被人奉为“二胡博士”。

吕文成演奏高胡
Lü Wencheng is playing the Gaohu

尹自重：梵铃王

尹自重（1903—1985），著名广东音乐小提琴演奏家、作曲家，原籍东莞，出生于顺德，旅居香港。尹自重在演奏“广东小提琴”方面饮誉全国，有“梵铃王”的美誉。尹自重是小提琴民族化的先驱，20世纪30年代，他第一个将小提琴引进广东音乐和粤剧音乐，按照广东的拉弦乐器演奏的基本规律，结合小提琴的演奏技法，创造一套广东音乐的演奏技法，改善乐队传统乐器音色不丰富、表现力不强的缺点。

尹自重 Yin Zizhong

techniques for Cantonese musical performance to enrich the tonality and expressive effects of the traditional Cantonese musical instruments.

He Dasha: Father of Jocular Songs

He Dasha (1896–1957), was born in an overseas Chinese family in Sanshui County of Guangdong Province. His original name is He Furu, but because of his funny performance, he was often nicknamed "He Dasha" in the Cantonese music circle. He Dasha was good at playing the guitar. He adapted the wood Hawaii guitar to fit the Cantonese music, and later the guitar became one of the common musical instruments in Cantonese music. He Dasha's musical performance was special and was often called "He style". He produced many Cantonese musical pieces with epochal features, including "A Peacock in His Pride", "Butterflies in the Flowers" and "Warblers in the Willows".

He Langping: Jack of All Trades

He Langping (1916–?), was born in Nanhai of Guangdong Province, and a famous player of Cantonese music good at playing various musical instruments. He became famous even when he was a boy. When he was 12, he often played Cantonese music on the harmonica, which was relayed by Guangzhou TV station. He dedicated all his life to Cantonese musical creation and performance. His musical works over the 50 years of his artistic life included "Spring in the Peach Groove", "Twin Swallows" and "Spring Celebration"; his dramatic works included *The Wedding*, *A Romance of the Western Chamber*, and *The Love Story of Liang Shanbo and Zhu Yingtai*.

何大傻：鬼马鼻祖

何大傻（1896—1957），出生于三水一个华侨家族，原名何福如。因其所唱之曲诙谐，而又多冠以“大傻”二字，故人称“何大傻”。何大傻擅长吉他，他把木制的“夏威夷”吉他广东化，使吉他成为广东音乐的常用的乐器之一。何大傻在粤曲演唱上独树“何腔”一帜，写过不少粤语时代曲，代表作有《孔雀开屏》《花间蝶》《柳底莺》等。

何大傻 He Dasha

何浪萍：多才多艺

何浪萍（1916—？），广东南海人，著名广东音乐演奏家，擅操各种乐器。他少年成名，12岁就多次在广州广播电视台表演口琴独奏广东音乐。他终身致力广东民间乐曲的创作和演奏，从艺五十多年来何浪萍创作的音乐作品有《春满桃园》《双飞燕》《庆春禧》等，戏剧作品有《结婚》《西厢记》《柳荫记》等40多个剧本。

MUSICAL WORKS OF EXCELLENCE

"PLANTAINS IN THE RAIN": A LINGNAN ROMANCE

This is one of the excellent musical pieces of early Cantonese music. It has a compact rhythm and is lyrical in nature, suitable to be sung to describe one's happiness as well as the poetic landscape and customs in Lingnan region. It gives the audience a sense of hearing the raindrops falling on the plantain leaves and reminds one of the dancing plantains as well as the happiness brought by good harvest.

"THE DRAGON BOAT RACE CHAMPION": PRIDE AND VIGOR

"The Dragon Boat Race Champion" was originally called "Racing Dragon Boats", the masterpiece of the master of Cantonese music He Liutang. "The Dragon Boat

名曲共赏

《雨打芭蕉》：南国情趣

广东音乐早期的优秀曲目之一，旋律紧密衔接、优美抒情，歌唱性很强，既流畅明快，表达了人们的喜悦之情，也展现了诗情画意般的岭南风光，犹如淅淅沥沥的雨点敲打着芭蕉，使人联想到芭蕉婆娑起舞之态，更使人想象到芭蕉丰收之后人们的喜悦之情。

《赛龙夺锦》：奋发向上

《赛龙夺锦》又名《龙舟竞渡》，是广东音乐名家何柳堂的代表作。《赛龙夺锦》原是一首丝竹乐曲，后来为了表现乐曲的气势，何柳堂将其改编为吹打乐合奏形式，增加了唢呐和打击乐器，使乐曲大为增色。全曲以高胡主奏，取材于广东五月端午人们赛龙舟的紧张、激烈场面，是一首有引子、尾声的单三部曲式结构的广东音乐。

Race Champion" was originally a musical piece played on stringed and wind musical instruments. Later, in order to produce the vigorous atmosphere, the ensemble of wind and percussion instruments were used. Especially, the use of suona and the percussion instruments made the music more sonorous. Gaohu is the major musical instrument. The scene it describes is the exciting scene when the local people hold dragon boat race during the Dragon Boat Festival. It adopts a three-part structure with an introduction and a coda.

《赛龙夺锦》描绘的情景
Scene of "The Dragon Boat Race Champion"

雨打芭蕉

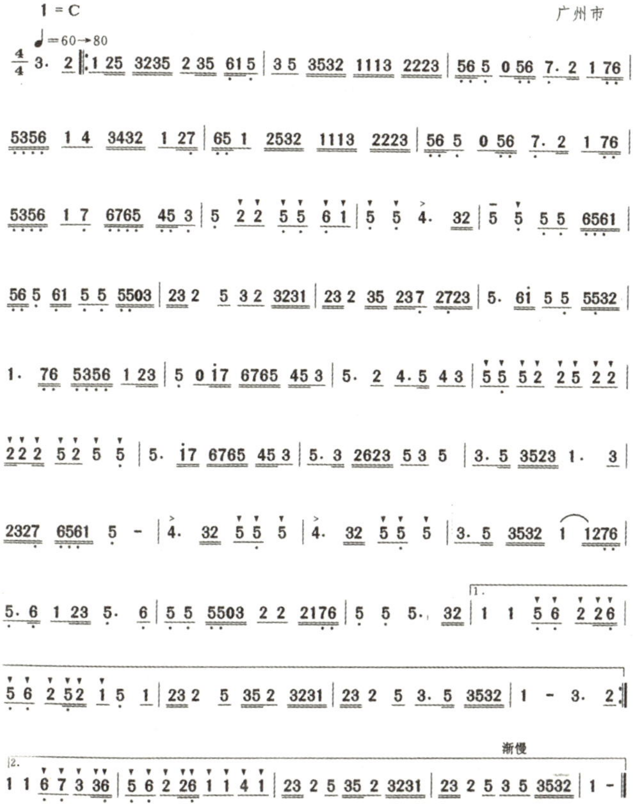

（沈　伟、李时成、陈春大、骆　津、陈添寿、何浪萍、黄家齐等演奏）

《中国民族民间器乐曲集成·广东卷》编辑部采录）

说明：1. 此曲流行于20世纪20年代前，乐谱载于丘鹤俦1917年编著的《弦歌必读》，并注明为“古谱”。另据传此谱原为何柳堂所传。

2. 所用乐器及定音：高胡 5 2 = $g^1 d^2$、二胡 1 5 = $c^1 g^1$、中胡 5 2 = g d^1、大阮 1 5 2 6 = C G d a、三弦 5 1 5 = G c g、秦琴 5 1 5 = g $c^1 g^1$、笛子筒音作 5 = g^1、扬琴 G—g^2。

《雨打芭蕉》乐谱

Music score for “Plantains in the Rain”

雨打芭蕉

扫描二维码
感受广东音乐

"STEP ON STEP": POPULAR EPOCHAL MUSIC

The title "Step on Step" is to imply the good opportunity to go higher and higher in the social ranks. Gaohu is used in two octaves to symbolize this good opportunity. In the early records of Cantonese music, Gaohu, piano, coconut-boxed erhu, pipa, and holed xiao were used together to make the audience feel excited and pleasant. A long portamento is produced by adaptations on Gaohu. The octave jumping made it sound fresh and novel.

"A PEACOCK IN HIS PRIDE": GUITAR MUSIC

He Dasha was unable to decide which musical instrument to use—guita or pipa—when he created "A Peacock in His Pride", so he provided two different drafts. But it proved that the one played on guitar was more popular than that played on pipa. Since then, this musical piece was always played mainly on guitar and was popular in many places of Guangdong.

"LITTLE TAOHONG":
BREAKING FREE FORM TRADITION

This is Yin Zizhong's musical masterpiece, which featured the innovative use of the violin in Cantonese music.

《步步高》：时代“流行曲”

《步步高》曲名寓意为“步步高升”，演奏时在两个八度音域中充分发挥高胡的技巧，给人以步步高升之感。在早期的唱片记录中，这首乐曲由高胡、钢琴、椰胡、琵琶、洞箫在一起合奏，整首乐曲具有活泼愉快的情绪，大段的滑音由高胡的技巧演变而来，其中出现八度大跳的旋律，让人耳目一新。

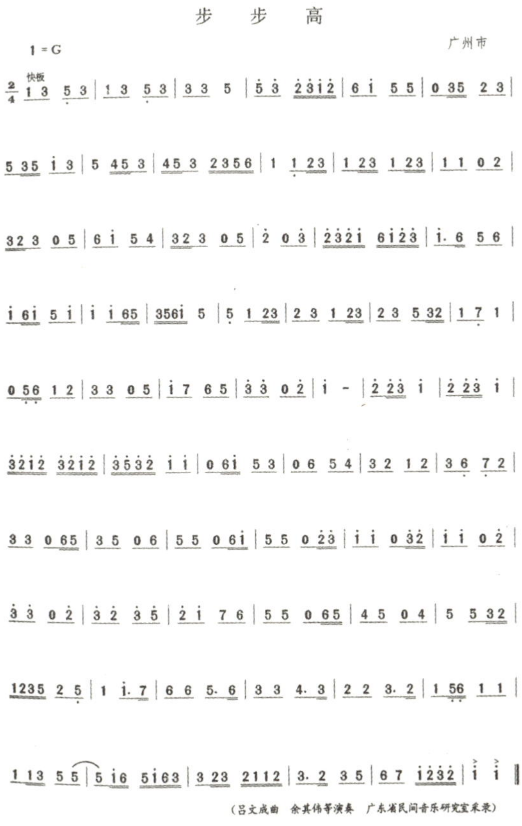

《步步高》乐谱 Music score for “Step on Step”

步步高

扫描二维码
感受广东音乐

"Little Taohong" was adapted from a traditional Cantonese music. The original musical piece featured slow rhythm and the pathetic air. Yin Zizhong raised the musical range by one octave, and added special portamentos. The musical piece after the adaptation sounded not melancholy, but brisk and gaudy.

孔雀开屏

扫描二维码
感受广东音乐

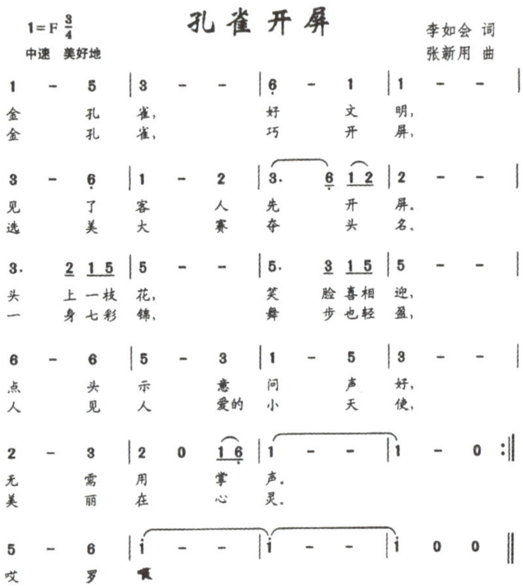

《孔雀开屏》乐谱

Music score for "A Peacock in His Pride"

Adviser of this Chapter: Chen Junhui (Director of Music Research Office of Guangdong Institute of Literature and Art)

《孔雀开屏》：吉他主打

何大傻当年创作出《孔雀开屏》，对于用吉他演奏好还是用琵琶演奏好，一时拿不定主意，便同时制作了两种版本。结果，吉他版的唱片销售量远远超越了琵琶版。现在的《孔雀开屏》还一直保持以吉他领奏的传统，在广东民间十分流行。

《小桃红》：突破传统

《小桃红》是尹自重的代表作，此曲开创了广东音乐的小提琴演奏风格。《小桃红》改编自一首传统粤曲，该曲节奏缓慢，情绪悲苦，尹自重在改编时将音域提高了一个八度，又加入具有特色的滑音，改编后的乐曲不再哀伤，听上去反而具有华丽、明亮的特点。

小桃红

扫描二维码
感受广东音乐

《小桃红》CD
A CD of "Little Taohong"

本章顾问：陈浚辉（广东省文艺研究所音乐研究室主任）

WORLD ON STAGE
—CANTONESE OPERA

Based on bangzi (Xipi in the Peking Opera) and erhuang, Cantonese opera, also known as the "Grand Opera" or "Guangdong Grand Drama", is a fusion of tunes of Guangdong's Haiyan, Yiyang, Kunshan, and bangzi, which flowed into Guangdong since the Ming and Qing Dynasties, and combined the elements of the folk music formed by the Pearl River Delta. It is formed in the Pearl River Delta region and is popular in Guangdong, Guangxi, Hong Kong and Macao while spreading far to Southeast Asia, America, Oceania, Europe and other overseas Chinese communities. It is the most influential and popular one of all the local operas.

Cantonese opera masters often travel to and from Guangzhou and Hong Kong to promote folk cultural exchanges. Located in Guangzhou, the Cantonese Opera Art Museum promotes the inheritance of Cantonese opera culture.

赏戏

粤剧

粤剧又称“大戏”或者“广东大戏”，是融汇明清以来流入广东的海盐、弋阳、昆山、梆子等诸腔并吸收珠江三角洲民间音乐所形成的以梆子（京剧称西皮）、二黄为主的我国南方一大剧种。它形成于珠江三角洲一带，流行于广东、广西、香港和澳门，远播东南亚、美洲、大洋洲、欧洲等华侨聚居地，是广东地方戏曲剧种中影响最大、流行最广的剧种。

粤剧名家经常往返广州、香港两地演出，推动了民间交流。粤剧艺术博物馆在广州建成，促进了粤剧文化的传承。

GRAND OPERA OF GUANGDONG

FROM QIONGHUA TO BAHE

In Guangdong and Guangxi, especially in the region of Pearl River Delta, there were already local opera troupes in the middle years of Ming Dynasty. During the reign of Emperor Jiaqing, a poet called Liang Xuyong from Nanhai County wrote in his "Fenjiang Folk Song": "Singing and dancing, a bustling life the performers create, /One after another, the red boats trail in the evening glow. /Year by year, the Heavenly Bliss Day visits, /When the multitude gather to watch Qionghua Show." Its description of the opera troupes and their performance told the reader the features of Cantonese opera in its early years: First, Cantonese opera developed to meet the demand of the local people to worship their gods during big ceremonies; second, the red boats were the moving camps of the local troupes; third, Qionghua Guild that was regarded as the trade organization of the local troupes had already appeared.

南粤大戏

从琼花到八和

两广尤其是珠三角地区，大约在明代中期已有成规模的本地戏班。嘉庆年间南海人梁序镛作有《汾江竹枝词》：“梨园歌舞赛繁华，一带红船泊晚沙。但到年年天贶节，万人围住看琼花。”这里对戏班表演场面的描写，说明早期粤剧有以下几个特点：一是粤剧产生于当地人传统祭祀场合唱戏酬神的需要；二是红船是本地戏班的流动营地；三是本地戏班的行业组织“琼花会馆”已经出现。

特别要提到的是红船。由于珠三角是著名水乡，内河密布交错，戏班以船只为载运工具，长年在各乡演出。在此期间，戏班服装道具存放、演员吃喝拉撒都在

清初“琼花水埗”石碑
Qionghua Wharf tablet in early Qing Dynasty

琼花会馆里供奉华光所使用的香炉
The incense burner kept in Qionghua Guild and used to worship Huaguang in the past

What needs to be mentioned is the red boat. Pearl River Delta was covered with numerous water courses. The local opera troupes used boats as their vehicle for their transportation when they staged performances. At that time, the costumes and stage properties of the troupes had to be stored on the boats, and the performers had to live on the boats. To make their troupes easy to be recognized and to attract audience, they painted their boats in red from prow to stern. So, their boats were called "red boats", and the troupe was called "Red Boat Troupe".

八和会馆
Bahe Guild

In 1854, the fourth year during the reign of Emperor Xianfeng in Qing Dynasty, a famous performer in Phoenix Troupe, a local opera troupe, who was called Li Wenmao, launched an uprising to echo Hong Xiuquan's Taiping Army. Later he was acclaimed as the king in Liuzhou of Guangxi Province. This caused Qing government to perscute vehemently the local opera troupes. Qionghua Guild wad destroyed, many performers were killed, and Cantonese opera was almost completely exterminated. After Taiping Army was completely defeated, the ban on Cantonese opera was finally lifted. With the permission of Ruilin, the governor of Guangdong and Guangxi provinces, the martial arts performer of Cantonese opera Kuang Xinhua collected money to rebuild the opera guild. Ten years' hard work witnessed the construction of Bahe Guild in Huangsha of Guangzhou in 1889, a guild to serve the trade of Cantonese opera.

李文茂雕塑
Statue of Li Wenmao

Bahe Guild provided a fair environment for the local

红船模型 Red boat model

船上。为了吸引乡民注意，船只通体涂成红色，因此被叫做“红船”。戏班演员也称自己为“红船子弟”。

清朝咸丰四年（1854年），本地班凤凰仪戏班老倌李文茂响应洪秀全太平军起义，后在广西柳州封王，引发清政府对本地戏班的残酷镇压，琼花会馆被拆毁，粤剧艺人被残杀，粤剧几遭火顶之灾。直至太平天国起义失败后，粤剧禁令松弛，当时著名的武生邝新华得到两广总督瑞麟的默许，筹款重建会馆。经过十年努力，1889年他在广州黄沙建成行业会馆——八和会馆。

八和会馆为本地班的订戏接戏提供良性竞争环境，又为单身艺人提供住所。八和会馆成立后，粤剧艺人队伍迅速壮大，到宣统元年（1909年），戏班数量多达1630家，这个时期在粤剧史上被称为“粤剧中兴”。

opera troupes to find customers and provided dwelling places for the performers. After Bahe Guild was established, the team of Cantonese opera performers developed rapidly. By the first year during the reign of Emperor Xuantong (1909), there were altogether 1630 troupes. This period was called the "Renaissance of Cantonese Opera".

FROM OFFICIAL LANGUAGE TO CANTONESE

Before the end of the 19th century, the earlier opera troupes used mainly the official language for their stage performances. In early years of the 20th century, the followers of Sun Yat-sen who supported the democratic revolution organized some theatrical societies of comrades to reform Cantonese opera performance as a tool to disseminate revolutionary ideas. They used the dialect in Guangzhou to stage performances, and many Cantonese opera troupes followed the fashion. With the practice by such famous Cantonese opera stars as Zhu Cibo, Qianli Ju, Baiju Rong, Liang Rong, the falsetto in Cantonese opera performance changed into real voice, the stage language for Cantonese opera performance changed from official language to Guangzhou dialect, which gave Cantonese opera its peculiar color and beauty.

陈少白（左三）与孙中山（左二）合影
Chen Shaobai (3rd from left) and Sun Yat-sen (2nd from left)

从官话到粤语

早期（19世纪末以前）本地戏班演唱用的是类似普通话的戏棚官话。20世纪初跟随孙中山支持民主革命的有识之士，创办了一批志士班改革戏剧，宣传革命。其中改用广州方言来演唱戏剧的尝试，使传统粤剧班纷纷效仿。经过名角朱次伯、千里驹、白驹荣、靓荣等不断实践尝试，粤剧得以完成声腔由“子喉”（假嗓）到“平喉”（真嗓）的最终转变。粤剧从官话过渡到粤方言之后，才开始真正形成本身的独特色彩和格调。

DECLINES AND RISES

Following its renaissance, Cantonese opera welcomed its peak of prosperity in the 1920s. There occurred companies that specialized in the management of opera troupes. There were tens of opera troupes with more than 100 performers. Many famous opera stars came to the audience's view who staged performance in Guangzhou and Hong Kong. These troupes were called the "Grand Troupe of Guangdong and Hong Kong". Cantonese opera was also very popular in Shanghai. During the Republic of China, the audience of Cantonese opera was only less than that of Peking opera. Five sects of Cantonese opera came into being, including "Xue (represented by Xue Juexian), Ma (represented by Ma Shizeng), Gui (represented by Gui Mingyang), Liao (represented by Liao Xiahuai) and Bai (represented by Baiju Rong)".

薛觉先剧照
Xue Juexian's stage photo

Sound films appeared in the end of 1920s and the 1930s, which exerted great impact on Cantonese opera market. As a result, many theatres were closed, and many Cantonese opera performers lost their jobs. The circle of Cantonese opera tried to produce films adapted from Cantonese opera classics, some opera classics were reformed, or they made use of the stage design or the excellent elements of other operas to earn a new life. Among them, the reformations by Xue Juexian and Ma Shizeng were the most influential, and in history, this was called "Xue-Ma Confront".

马师曾剧照
Ma Shizeng's stage photo

几度兴衰

粤剧中兴后，在20世纪20年代达到鼎盛时期。当时出现专营戏班的公司，拥有一百来号艺人的大型戏班多达数十个，其中名角众多，往返广州和香港两地演出，被称为“省港大班”。粤剧在上海也大受欢迎，民国期间上海粤剧的观众人数仅次于京剧。这个时期粤剧产生“薛（薛觉先）、马（马师曾）、桂（桂名扬）、廖（廖侠怀）、白（白驹荣）” 五大流派。

20世纪20年代末到30年代，有声电影兴起，对粤剧演出市场造成极大冲击，戏院停业，大批伶人失业。粤剧界通过拍摄粤剧电影、改良剧本、舞美设计、吸收兄弟戏剧特长等改革自救，其中以

《帝女花》 The Floral Princess

In the following 14 years' War of Resistance against Japan, China suffered depression in almost every trade. After the founding of the People's Republic of China, a reform in the theatrical circle was launched. The looked-down-upon performers turned into respected "workers of art". Many excellent plays were produced, including *Searching the Academy*, *Guan Hanqing* and *Stories of the Mountain Village*.

Since the 1980s, Cantonese opera has experienced a revival and become a prosperous trade. In the face of different cultures, contemporary Cantonese opera performers should boldly carry out reforms and innovation. In 2003, Cantonese Opera Troupe of Guangzhou adapted and produced the aesthetic play *Tragedy of Flower and Moon* which featured delicate stage design, elegant melodies and musical accompaniment with popular elements. In 2015, Guangdong Theatre of Cantonese Opera worked together with the working team of "JX Online 3" to produce the first innovative play *Duel at Tiance Palazzo* in the form of online game plus Cantonese opera, which provided Cantonese opera the epochal glamour. These innovations attracted a lot of young men to Cantonese opera.

薛（左）马（右）合影
Xue Juexian (left) and Ma Shizeng (right)

In March 2012, in order to implement the requirements of Guangzhou municipal Party committee and government on building a world famous historical and cultural city and promoting the development of Cantonese Opera, the Cantonese Opera museum project was officially launched. The project is a key cultural construction project

《山乡风云》*Stories of the Mountain Village*

薛觉先和马师曾改革影响力最大，粤剧史上称之为“薛马争雄”。

全面抗日战争期间，百业萧条，直到新中国成立后，开展戏曲改革运动，“戏子”变为“文艺工作者”，社会地位大大提高，也产生了一批《搜书院》《关汉卿》《山乡风云》等优秀剧目。

20世纪80年代到今天，粤剧从复苏到兴旺。面对多元文化的冲击，当代粤剧人积极面对，紧贴时代潮流进行创新。2003年广州粤剧团编排了时尚唯美粤剧《花月影》，舞美设计精雕细琢，曲辞优雅上口，音乐添加流行元素，令人耳目一新。2015年广东粤剧院与热门网游“剑网3”合作，出品“网游+粤剧”《决战天策府》，赋予粤剧时代魅力。这些创新无不吸引大批年轻人重新走入戏院观看粤剧。

in Guangzhou. After many investigations, the Cantonese Opera museum is located in the north of Enning Road, south of Yuanhe street and west of Duobao square in Liwan District, surrounded by historical and cultural relics such as Bahe Guild, Taihua Building, Baoqing Pawnshop, Li Xiaolong's ancestral residence.

After its completion, Cantonese Opera museum is a Chinese garden style museum with Lingnan style and water town characteristics. It is divided into two sides along Lizhi Bay. On June 9, 2016, it was officially opened to the public. The garden center of the museum is equipped with an antique stage, which regularly holds performances of Cantonese Songs and Opera every week to dynamically display the artistic characteristics of Cantonese Opera. The completion of Cantonese Opera museum also makes this area a Grand View Park of Cantonese opera art and culture in Xiguan, and a museum without walls to display Cantonese opera art and Lingnan culture.

GUANGDONG-HONG KONG-MACAO GREATER BAY COMMUNICATION

After the founding of the People's Republic of China, many famous Cantonese opera performers staged performances in both Guangzhou and Hong Kong, and the plays staged and the troupes were almost the same. In the 1950s, Cantonese opera in Hong Kong turned its focus back into the language, melody and characterization of the plays. Famous performer

2012年3月，为落实广州市委、市政府关于建设世界历史文化名城、促进粤剧艺术事业发展的要求，粤剧艺术博物馆项目正式启动。该项目是广州市的重点文化建设项目。经多方考察后，粤剧艺术博物馆定址于荔湾区恩宁路以北、元和街以南、多宝坊以西地段，周边有八和会馆、泰华楼、宝庆大押、李小龙祖居等历史建筑。

建成后的粤剧艺术博物馆是一座具有岭南风格、水乡特色的中国园林式博物馆，沿荔枝湾涌分为南北两岸。2016年6月9日，正式向公众开放。博物馆园林中心设有仿古戏台，每周定期举行粤剧粤曲展演，动态展示粤剧艺术特色。粤剧艺术博物馆的建成，也使这一片区成为西关粤剧艺术文化大观园，形成一座展示粤剧艺术和岭南文化的、没有围墙的博物馆。

吉庆别馆，位于粤剧艺术博物馆
Jiqing Annexe, located in Cantonese Opera Museum

such as Bai Xuexian, Ren Jianhui, and famous playwright Tang Disheng together produced many classical plays such as *The Princess' Love* and *The Story of Purple Hairpin*, which brought Cantonese opera to a higher level.

Till today, Macao still keeps the tradition of staging performances to worship gods. Before the birthday of Goddess Mazu every year, the people of Macao will build temporary stages and invite the troupes of Guangdong, Guangxi and Hong Kong to stage performances. Building a temporary stage to stage Cantonese opera performances is still kept in Macao and Hong Kong today.

In 2002, Guangdong, Hong Kong and Macao began to work together with an attempt to put Cantonese opera on the list intangible cultural heritages. After eight years' hard work, Cantonese opera was listed among the group of intangible cultural heritages. Since then, the cultural communication between the different places of the Greater Bay Area becomes common.

DISSEMINATION

Southeast Asia is called the second hometown of Cantonese opera. In the middle of the 19th century, there had already occurred in Singapore the trade organization of Cantonese opera called "Li Yuan Tang". The famous Cantonese opera performers in the 20th century such as Xue Juexian, Ma Shizeng, Chen Feinong were all very popular in Malaysia and Singapore. The Gold Rush in the 19th century

粤港澳大湾区交流

新中国成立之前，粤剧名伶往返广州、香港两地演出，剧目题材几乎完全相同，戏班也没有广州、香港之分。香港粤剧在20世纪50年代后期回归艺术本身，注重曲辞、音律和人物的思想塑造，以名伶白雪仙、任剑辉，名编剧唐涤生为代表创作演出一批如《帝女花》《紫钗记》等优秀作品，把粤剧推向更高的艺术层次。

澳门到现在依旧保留唱戏酬神的传统。每年妈祖诞期前后，澳门就会搭大棚作为临时舞台，聘请两广和香港不同的戏班前来演出。搭棚唱戏这种传统粤剧演出方式，在澳门和香港至今得到保存和延续。

从2002年开始，粤港澳三地更是联合进行粤剧申遗工作，经过八年努力，申遗成功，标志着大湾区的文化交流更加紧密，不可分割。

2017年11月，粤剧《辛弃疾》在澳门文化中心首演

The first show of Cantonese opera *Xin Qiji* in Macao Cultural Center in November, 2017

1905年，马来西亚怡保文明粤剧慈善班
Yibao Wenming, the Cantonese opera charity troupe in Malaysia in 1905

attracted many Chinese people in Guangdong Province to the United States, and Cantonese opera also went there with these Chinese emigrants. For the past century, many troupes went to the overseas Chinese communities in the United States to stage performances, and the overseas Chinese there also organized their own professional and amateur Cantonese opera troupes, which promoted the dissemination of Cantonese opera in the world. Beginning with 1990, the Cantonese opera troupes in Guangdong, Hong Kong, Macao, Asia, America and Europe meet in Guangzhou every four years to take part in the Guangzhou International Cantonese Opera Festival. The festival in 2016 attracted 143 opera troupes in 20 countries and regions of the world, which won Cantonese opera a greater fame.

香远益清

南洋被称为粤剧的“第二故乡”。19世纪中叶新加坡已经出现粤剧的行业组织“梨园堂”，20世纪的粤剧名伶如薛觉先、马师曾、陈非侬等在马来西亚、新加坡等地都大受欢迎。19世纪美国淘金热吸引大批粤籍华人赴美，粤剧跟随传入美洲。一个世纪以来，戏班到美国华侨居住地不断演出，当地华侨也自己成立戏班和业余社团，推动粤剧在海外传播。

从1990年开始，粤港澳三地、亚洲、美洲、欧洲等地的粤剧团每四年一次聚集羊城，参加“羊城国际粤剧节”，相互交流。2016年的第七届粤剧节，已经吸引了来自20多个国家和地区的143个粤剧社团参加，大大提高了粤剧的国际声誉。

羊城国际粤剧节

Guangzhou International Cantonese Opera Festival

ARTS OF CANTONESE OPERA

SINGING STYLES

The tune of Cantonese opera combines the singing styles of the local operas such as bangzi and erhuang. Bangzi is characterized by its sonorous sound and brisk rhythm, while erhuang by its gentle and slow rhythm. Because of this, there was a saying in the circle of Chinese opera: "Bangzi is sung for bustling topics, while erhuang is sung when it is melancholy." At the beginning years of Xinhai Revolution, the societies of comrades that sang for revolutionary ideas first changed the stage language, replacing the official language that was similar to Mandarin with the dialect of Guangzhou and replacing the falsetto with real voice, which was followed by the changes in pitches, movements and changes in the use of different singing styles. The single melody was replaced by the free use of different melodies used in bangzi, erhuang, xipi, paizi and ditties as well as those used Lingnan arts like Nanyin

唱念做打

唱腔特色

粤剧声腔是梆子、二黄并蓄。梆子音调爽朗明快，二黄音调缠绵委婉，故有句戏谚叫做“行路唱梆子，落难叹二黄”。辛亥革命初期，宣扬革命的粤剧志士戏班率先改变演唱语言，从戏棚官话（近似普通话）变为粤方言，嗓音由“子喉”（假嗓）转换为“平

采南歌班培训地海幢寺

Hoi Tong Monastery, the training centre of Cainan Troupe

opera, Muyu opera, Dragon Boat opera, and also elements from popular songs, foreign songs. All these changes diversified the singing styles of Cantonese opera.

SHACK FACE

高边锣
Broad-edge gong

"Shack face" is the name for the musical bands of Cantonese opera. It is called so because the musical bands of the traditional Cantonese opera were often stationed in the center of the stage where they could be seen by the audience once they entered the theatre. The number of players in the musical band in the early years was usually 10; later there were often 13 people and the center of the musical band was the drum master.

In its early years, drums and gongs were the soul of Cantonese opera. In the rural area, the performance was usually done in the open place where the temporary stage was built for the performance. To attract the audience, drums and gongs were often used. After the singing style changed, the musical instruments used by shack face also underwent changes. The hard-bow combination in the age when bangzi and erhuang dominated turned into the soft-bow combination represented by Gaohu. Later, with the frequent communication of the Cantonese opera troupes with the artistic groups in the foreign countries, the western musical instruments were introduced into the musical bands of Cantonese opera. Saxophone characterized by its broad

喉”（真嗓），调高、旋律、运腔方法也随之发生改变。单一旋律（一线到底）的规矩被打破，一个唱段里梆子、二黄、西皮、牌子、小曲等自由穿插，岭南民间说唱艺术如南音、木鱼、龙舟等。电影流行曲、外国歌曲等皆被吸收，丰富了粤剧唱法。

大戏棚面

棚面是粤剧乐队及其成员的传统称呼，因为传统粤剧全部乐队皆位于舞台中央，进场观众第一眼就能看到，故称“棚面”。棚面早期十人，后改制为十三人，掌板是乐队核心。

早期锣鼓是粤剧的灵魂，乡下演出的戏班多在空旷处搭棚，依靠锣鼓来招揽观众。唱法改变后，棚面乐器也发生变化，从梆子二黄时代的硬弓组合，转为高胡为主的软弓组合。再后来粤剧戏团海外交流频繁，西洋乐器也被纳入乐队伴奏中来。萨克斯风由于音域较广，伴奏时容易融入粤剧传统音乐，因而成为乐队最喜爱的音乐伴奏乐器。

十大行当

粤剧早期表演行当仿照的是汉剧戏班的行当建制，分为末、净、生、旦、丑、外、小、贴、夫、杂十大行当。清末民初，再细分为25种。“朝廷论爵，戏班论位”，行当排列次序要求严格，互相不能逾越或庖代。1918年前后出现“文武生”，随后跨行当演出

tone range was introduced into Cantonese opera for musical accompaniment and became the most favorite instrument in the musical bands.

TEN ROLES

The roles for Cantonese opera performers in the early years followed the classification of Han opera, including mo, jing, sheng, dan, chou, wai, xiao, tie, fu, za, ten roles altogether. At the turn of Qing Dynasty and the Republic of China, the roles were re-divided into 25 kinds. "There are different roles in the opera troupe as there are different ranks in the royal court." Every role had its own position. Overstepping was not allowed. Around 1918, there occurred the role called wen wu sheng, and later the performance that overstepped different roles became common. Xue Juexian, for example, could play xiao sheng, xiao wu, hua dan and chou sheng also; Ma Shizeng was known for his chou sheng performance and he also played the roles of wen wu sheng and hua dan. Under the impact of films, radio station in the early years of the 20th century, "six-pillar-role" system came into being which was designed to reduce the number of performers in a performance to reduce the cost. This system meant that six pillar roles played other roles in a stage performance besides his or her major roles. They had to master various performing skills and play other roles on the stage.

"六柱制"海报
Playbill for "six-pillar-role system" performance

末 Mo

净 Jing

生 Sheng

旦 Dan

丑 Chou

外 Wai

小 Xiao

贴 Tie

夫 Fu

杂 Za

COSTUME AND STAGECRAFT

The traditional Cantonese opera featured simple stagecraft where a table and two chairs could imitate all kinds of scenes, sometimes with such explanatory words as "river side" or "mountain", etc. During the Republic of China, in order to attract the audience, the stage background became more and more beautiful and complicated, usually including large-scale painting, cubic models to serve the performance. For example, there was craftsman standing in water; there was also small train running on the stage. Besides, light, electric devices and other technologies were used to produce glamourous stage background. The traditional costumes in Cantonese opera usually used complicated and bright Cantonese embroidery. Later, for the special light effect, the imported tiny plastic pieces, pearls, metallic pieces, even small light bulbs were used to decorate the costumes. The exotic costumes could easily attract the attention of the audience, but at the same time they damaged the artistic effect of Cantonese opera. So, since the 1950s, those exotic stagecrafts that deviated from the tradition of Cantonese opera had been discarded.

粉色密片男蟒袍
Costume for the role of high officials

民国时期的粤剧舞台布景
Stage scene of Cantonese opera during the Republic of China

成了风气，薛觉先小生、小武、花旦、丑生都能演，马师曾演丑生出名，又兼文武生和花旦。20世纪初，粤剧受到电影、电台冲击，为了压缩演员人数，节约成本，“六柱制”应运而生。它是指六个台柱支撑一个戏班的演出，每个演员除了自己本来的行当外，还要掌握多种表演手段和技艺，兼演其他行当的戏。

舞美服饰

传统粤剧舞台设置朴实，一桌两椅可以模拟所有场景地点，最多再加上“河边”“高山”等简洁的文字说明。民国时期，为了吸引观众，舞台背景开始变得华丽繁复，通过大型绘画、立体造型等为剧中人物打造特定场景，如艺人站在水里表演，还把小型火车开上舞台。此外也借助光、电、化等新科技制作灿烂夺目的灯光背景和机关背景。传统粤剧服饰采用技艺精湛、色泽鲜艳的广绣，后为了让戏服有流光溢彩的效果，还添加进口的胶片、珠筒、金属片甚至小灯泡。奇装异服容易抓住观众眼球，但也因此削弱粤剧的艺术表现力。故20世纪50年代以后，一些背离粤剧艺术表演宗旨的舞美服饰已经消失。

古代将军戏服（胶片男扣仔）
Costume for the role of general

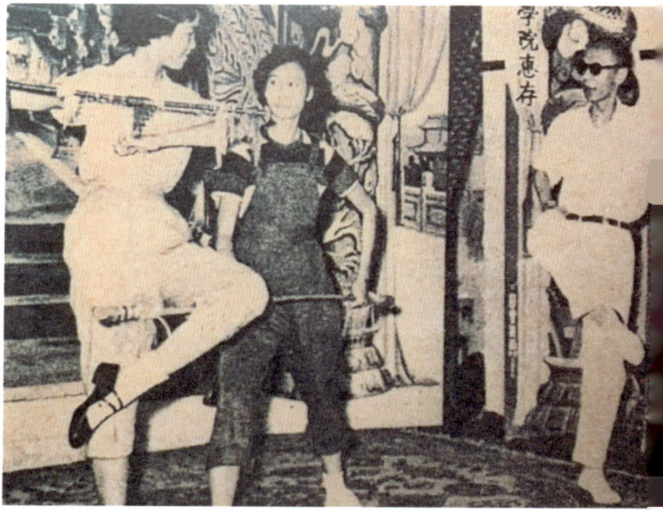

演员练习对枪 Performers practicing spears

STAGE TRICKS

踩砂煲
Stepping on clay pots

What is special about the martial performance in Cantonese opera is its use of the "real fight", namely the use of real kung fu and real weapons. The forefather of the "real fight" were Zhishan, the chan master of Shaolin Temple and the layman monk Hong Xiguan. They taught the Cantonese opera performers with kung fu such as "wood figures", "wood rods" and "luohan boxing" that the martial monks usually learned. The opera performers made adaptations to these kung fu tricks to suit the stage performance. The most famous stage tricks that are still used now include "stepping on clay pot", "face change", "teeth trick", "blood spitting", "stilt walking", "mirror looking", and "five-item combat".

功夫绝技

粤剧的武戏特色是“打真军”，即以真功夫、真兵器入戏。师祖是福建泉州南少林寺的至善禅师和其俗家弟子洪熙官，他们把教习武僧的训练方法和传统套路，如“木人桩”“六点半棍法”“十八罗汉伏虎拳”等传授给戏班子弟，戏班再根据这些套路演化适合舞台表演的功夫特技。出名的有“踩砂煲”“变脸”“耍牙”“踩跷”“照镜”“打五件”等。

耍牙 Teeth trick

高台照镜 Mirror looking at high table

DIVERSE PLAYS ON STAGE

There are as many as 11000 plays in Cantonese opera, the biggest number among different kinds of operas. The subject matters for Cantonese opera are diversified, absorbing diverse cultural and artistic elements of Chinese and foreign arts, with ever-changing contents and artistic techniques. The source of the plays of Cantonese opera can be divided into three types: first, the Nan operas in Song and Yuan dynasties, plays in Yuan and Ming dynasties, romance stories in Ming and Qing dynasties, such as *The Romance of West Chamber*, *The Orphan of the Zhaos*; second, the 18 classical plays, the new 18 classical plays, the grand 18 classical plays; third, folklores, local legends, and unofficial

传统剧目《六国大封相》
Traditional play: *Prime Minister of Six States*

《紫钗记》 *The Story of Purple Hairpin*

海纳百川

粤剧剧目数量众多，达11000多个，堪称戏剧界世界之最。而且它题材广泛、海纳百川，吸收古今中外优秀文化艺术，思想内容和编剧手法与时俱进。粤剧的传统剧目来源：一是宋元南戏、元明杂剧、明清传奇，如《西厢记》《搜孤救孤》等；二是“江湖十八本”“新江湖十八本”“大排场十八本”等；三是民间传说、地方掌故、稗官野史，如《梁天来》《王大儒供状》等。

传统粤剧没有专门的剧本，为提纲戏，演员依照提纲自由发挥。20世纪30年代开始出现专职编剧，自此粤剧产量剧增。著名的编剧有南海十三郎，他为薛觉先写的《心声泪影》《燕归人未归》《寒江钓雪》等名剧轰动一时。20世纪50年代编剧唐涤生为任剑辉、白雪仙“仙凤鸣”剧团创作的剧本《帝女花》《再世红

histories, such as *Liang Tianlai* and *Wang Daru's Written Confession*.

The traditional Cantonese opera had no specific plays. The traditional plays were just outlines by which the performers staged performance spontaneously with their free imagination. In the 1930s, professional playwrights appeared, and from then on, the number of plays of Cantonese opera increased greatly. The famous playwright included the Nanhai Thirteenth Son who produced such famous plays as *A Pathetic Love*, *The Swallow Came back without the Lover*, *Reunion* and *Fishing in the Snow* for Xue Juexian. In the 1950s, Tang Disheng created for Ren Jianhui and Bai Xuexian's "Phoenix Troupe" such classical plays as *The Princess' Love*, *Love in the Red Chamber* and *The Story of Purple Hairpin*. Besides, playwrights and famous opera stars also cooperated to produce such well-known plays as *The Women's Grudge*, *Pity the Poor Girl*, *Searching the Academy* and *Guan Hanqing*.

梅记》《紫钗记》等至今仍是经典。此外编剧、名伶合力创作的《客途秋恨》《苦凤莺怜》《搜书院》《关汉卿》等一批著名剧目也影响深远。

20世纪50年代，马师曾、红线女主演《关汉卿》剧照

Stage photo of *Guan Hanqing* starring by Ma Shizeng and Hung Sin-nui in the 1950s

SINGING STYLES AND MASTERS

QIANLI JU AND JU STYLE

Qianli Ju (1886–1936), was born in Shunde of Guangdong and one of the famous hua dan player. For the first time in the trade of hua dan, he tried to sing in real voice with the everyday language and reform the tube instruments. During performance, he put all his heart in to feel what the characters he played might feel. In cases of tragic scenes, he often wept violently himself. And because of this, he was often called as the "master of tragedy". His masterpieces included *Golden-Leaved Chrysanthemum*, *Swallow Attic* and *New Birth*.

LIANG YUANHENG AND PRECISE HENG

Liang Yuanheng (1892–1964), was born in Heshan of Guangdong Province and was often nicknamed as "Jack-of-All-Trade Xiao Wu Sheng" . He learned from Zhou Yuli and was

名伶名腔

“驹腔”千里驹

千里驹 Qianli Ju

千里驹（1886—1936），广东顺德人，著名花旦王。在旦行中首先尝试以白话唱平喉，改革喉管乐器。在表演时注重全身心投入，设身处地感受剧中人物情感，演到动情处悲痛欲绝，不能自已，故而被称作“悲剧圣手”。代表作有《金叶菊》《燕子楼》《再生缘》等。

“寸度亨”靓元亨

靓元亨 Liang Yuanheng

靓元亨（1892—1964），广东鹤山人，人称“全才小武”，师从小武周瑜利，唱作俱佳。他在《凤仪亭》里扎架时创造了四个

famous for his singing and martial arts on the stage. During the performance in the famous play *Dating at Fengyi Pavilion*, he presented four different postures on the stage, which was called "Lü Bu Posture", and was often used in this trade. Liang Yuanheng paid great attention to the images of the characters in the play, and created the famous image of Wu Song in the plays singing about the heroic figure Wu Song. And because of this he was often called as the "living Wu Song". He had another nickname—"Precise Heng", because his postures and body movements were all very precise, as if everything was measured by a ruler.

XUE JUEXIAN AND XUE STYLE

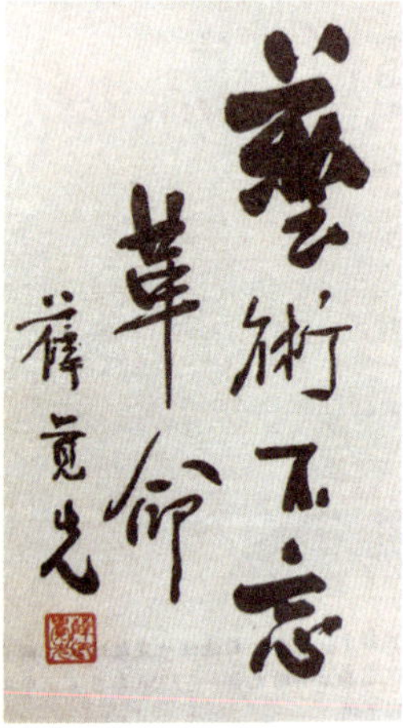

薛觉先题字
Inscription by Xue Juexian

Xue Juexian (1904–1956), was from Shunde of Guangdong Province, but he was born in Hong Kong. Xue Juexian first learned to play the role of clowns, but was known for his role of wen wu sheng plus that of dan. He could play different roles, so that he was often called "Master Jack of All Trades". He was dedicated to the reform of Cantonese opera, good at absorbing excellent elements of other local operas and arts. He reformed the costumes of Cantonese opera, making-up techniques, stage scene, musical accompaniment and play writing to enrich the art of Cantonese opera. Xue Juexian also tried new forms of arts. He ever produced the film *White Golden Dragon*, and cooperated with the playwright to create the classical plays like *Why Not Return*, *The Girls*, *Sisters in Law*. He also produced new musical pieces and invented his special singing style "Xue

功架，架式多变、造型俊美，被称为“吕布架”，一直为行内沿用；他认真研究剧中人物性格，演出生动，在武松系列剧里塑造的武松形象，被戏迷称为“生武松”。靓元亨还有一个外号叫“寸度亨”，特指他的动作、手势分寸之准确，好比用尺量过一样，没有半点多余。

“薛腔”薛觉先

薛觉先 Xue Juexian

薛觉先（1904—1956），广东顺德人，出生在香港。薛觉先学过丑角，以文武生出名，又可反串旦角，戏路很广，被称为“万能泰斗”。他致力推行粤剧改革，善于借鉴其他地方戏剧和艺术门类的特长，对粤剧从服饰、化妆、布景、音乐伴奏到编剧都进行全方位革新，丰富了粤剧艺术。薛觉先还不断尝试新的艺术形式，如拍摄电影《白金龙》，与编剧合作编写出经典剧目《胡不归》《女儿香》《姑缘嫂劫》，还创作新的乐曲旋律，自创的“薛腔”及“问字攞腔”的演唱技巧，成为后来粤剧演员的要诀。

薛觉先抗日爱国剧《貂蝉》
Xue Juexian's anti-Japanese play *Diaochan*

Style" featuring clear line reading, sonorous voice, easy rhythm, which became a principle that Cantonese opera performers followed for practice.

MA SHIZENG AND MA STYLE

Ma Shizeng (1900–1964), was born in Shunde of Guangdong. When he was young, he was sold to Southeast Asia and was once an apprentice, did jobs like waiter, mineworker, and other strenuous jobs. All these experiences proved to be the fountainhead for his later stage performance. He imitated the calling of the roadside sellers and formed his unique singing style nicknamed as the "beggar call" which featured singing together with asides and was very funny. And because of this, he was called the "King of Clowns". Ma Shizeng was once the pioneer of Cantonese opera reform. He took Guangzhou dialect into Cantonese opera, changing its official language into everyday language. He was also the first who changed the all-male troupes into those including both male and female performers, the first to use the western musical instruments in musical accompaniment, and the first who used only the western musical instruments for the musical accompaniment in Cantonese opera. His boldness in reforming Cantonese opera won him the name the "New Play Giant".

BAIJU RONG AND BAI STYLE

Baiju Rong (1892–1974), was born in Shunde of

“马腔”马师曾

马师曾 Ma Shizeng

马师曾（1900—1964），广东顺德人，年轻时生活坎坷，卖身南洋，从事过学徒、伙计、矿工、苦力等多个底层行业，这些经历为他的粤剧表演提供了源于生活的灵感。他独创的“乞儿喉”，就是借鉴街边小贩叫卖声，半唱半白，特点鲜明，也因此被誉为“丑生之王”。马师曾是粤剧改革的猛将，他将粤方言入曲，完成粤剧从戏棚官话到白话的转变。他第一个将戏班从全男班改为男女合班，在乐队伴奏中引进西洋乐器，甚至全用西洋乐器伴奏。马师曾大刀阔斧地改革，被誉为“新剧巨子”。

《搜书院》 *Searching the Academy*

Guangdong to a family with Cantonese opera traditions. He was known for the role of the emperor he played in the play *New Birth*, and was therefore often called the "King of Xiao Sheng". Baiju Rong dedicated himself to replacing the official language on the stage with Guangzhou dialect. He invented his own singing style which was called "Bai Style". Baiju Rong became blind at his mid age, but he still could judge the position he should stand on the stage with the help of the crisscrossed bamboo sticks put underneath the carpet and finish his performance perfectly. And this won him the nickname "the Pavel Korchagin in Chinese Opera".

HUNG SIN-NUI AND HONG STYLE

Hung Sin-nui (1924–2013), was born in Kaiping of Guangdong to a family with Cantonese opera tradition. At the age of 17, she began to play the role of zheng yin hua dan and invented her singing style "Hong Style". She ever cooperated with Ma Shizeng, Xue Juexian in such classical plays as *Pity the Poor Girl*, *Madame Butterfly*, *Guan Hanqing*, *Searching the Academy*, and *A History of Royal Hate in Qing Dynasty*, and created such classical theatrical figures as Cui Lian, Wang Zhaojun, Li Xiangjun. After the founding of the People's Republic of China, she was appointed heads in Cantonese Opera Troupe of Guangdong, Guangdong Theatre of Cantonese Opera, and the "Hung Sin-nui Art Centre", and organized the "Hung Sin-nui Training Foundation", dedicating herself to the domestic artistic communication and cultivation of Cantonese opera talents.

Adviser of this Chapter: Zhang Jinqiong (Vice president of Guangdong Opera Academy)

“白腔”白驹荣

白驹荣 Baiju Rong

白驹荣（1892—1974），广东顺德人，粤剧世家出身，因扮演《再生缘》里的皇帝而走红，被誉为“小生王”。白驹荣致力推广用粤方言代替戏棚官话，发展出自己独特的唱腔“白腔”。他中年失明，但仍能凭借舞台经验，依靠舞台地毯下的十字竹片来辨明方位，精湛地完成表演，被田汉誉为“中国的保尔•柯察金”。

“红腔”红线女

红线女 Hung Sin-nui

红线女（1924—2013），广东开平人，出身粤剧世家，17岁开始担任正印花旦，独创“红腔”，与马师曾、薛觉先合作过《苦凤莺怜》《蝴蝶夫人》《关汉卿》《搜书院》《清宫恨史》等经典剧目，塑造翠莲、王昭君、李香君等多个光彩照人的形象。新中国成立后，红线女先后在广东粤剧团、广东粤剧院、红线女艺术中心担任职务，并成立基金会，致力国内艺术交流和粤剧人才的培养。

本章顾问：张晋琼（广东省粤剧院副院长）

LINGNAN CULTURE
YOUTH BOOK

岭南文化青年读本

STARTING FROM GUANGZHOU

从广州出发

下册

共青团广州市委员会　编

南方日报出版社
NANFANG DAILY PRESS
中国·广州

图书在版编目（CIP）数据

岭南文化青年读本. 下册 / 共青团广州市委员会 编. -- 广州 : 南方日报出版社, 2019.10

ISBN 978-7-5491-2081-9

Ⅰ. ①岭… Ⅱ. ①共… Ⅲ. ①地方文化—广东—青年读物 Ⅳ. ①G127.65-49

中国版本图书馆 CIP 数据核字（2019）第 223544 号

LINGNAN WENHUA QINGNIAN DUBEN

岭南文化青年读本（下册）

编　　者：共青团广州市委员会
出版发行：南方日报出版社
地　　址：广州市广州大道中 289 号
出 版 人：周山丹
责任编辑：刘志一　李佳航
封面设计：肖晓文
责任技编：王　兰
责任校对：魏智宏
经　　销：全国新华书店
印　　刷：广州岭美文化科技有限公司
开　　本：889mm×1194mm　1/32
印　　张：3.75
字　　数：210 千字
版　　次：2019 年 10 月第 1 版
印　　次：2019 年 10 月第 1 次印刷
定　　价：68.00 元（全两册）

投稿热线：（020）87360640　读者热线：（020）87363865

发现印装质量问题，影响阅读，请与承印厂联系调换。

目 录

CONTENTS

CRAFTSMANSHIP
—LINGNAN ARCHITECTURE

Lingnan architecture is one important part of Lingnan culture. The diversity of Lingnan culture enables Lingnan architecture to borrow the cultural elements of Central China, cultures of other regions and even those of foreign cultures while inheriting those of the local culture. Different ages produced different architecture. From the traditional architecture, modern western architecture, hybrid architecture, national architecture to modern new architecture, Lingnan architecture always features rich diversity in its forms.The city buildings in Guangzhou take in the technology and styles of the western architecture, which is something pioneering.

匠心

岭南建筑

岭南建筑是岭南文化的重要组成部分。岭南文化的多元性使岭南建筑的风格既有承袭中原文化、借鉴其他地域文化和海外文化的一面，又有保持本土文化特色的一面。不同时期的时代背景造就不同时期的岭南建筑，从早期的传统建筑、近代的西式建筑、折中建筑、民族建筑到现代的新建筑，建筑呈现出多样化的独特形态。广州城市建筑在吸收西方建筑技术和风格的基础上，领风气之先。

INCLUSIVENESS

INDEPENDENT DEVELOPMENT

Because of the geographical restriction, the ridges in South China blocked the traffic from Lingnan to Central China, the influences of Confucian culture in Central China on Lingnan was limited. This enabled Lingnan to form an independent cultural system, which provided opportunities for this region to develop its own culture. Land traffic was blocked, but the traffic on the sea was convenient. With the development of maritime trade, Lingnan enjoyed opportunities that inland China did not have. In its years of foreign trade, this region absorbed the foreign cultures, and its architecture was thereby given features different from those in North China.

兼容并包

自我发展

由于地域限制，五岭阻隔了岭南到中原的交通，中原儒家文化对岭南的影响有限。这使得岭南在历史进程中形成一套独立的文化系统，地域特色有了展示和自我发展空间。陆路交通受阻，海上交

余荫山房 Yuyin Garden

番禺宝墨园 Baomo Garden • Panyu

陈家祠廊道
Corridor of the Chen Clan Ancestral Hall

PRACTICALITY

Lingnan climate is hot, humid and rainy. Therefore, the traditional buildings in Lingnan region are often exquisite, open and air-permeable to fit the local natural environment, enjoying good ventilation, heat insulation, sun protection and damp proof. Foreign architecture also has to adapt to the climate in this region. For example, the distances between two buildings are shortened to reduce the time for people to walk in the hot sun. Besides, some buildings use a lot of ventilation devices, such as corridors to create a microclimate environment to avoid the heat and humidity. Flexible designs are used for the buildings while practicality is taken into consideration.

通顺畅。随着海上贸易的繁荣发展，岭南又较内陆开风气之先。长期对外贸易中对外来文化的兼容吸收，也形成了岭南建筑区别于北方建筑的特有风格。

务实致用

岭南气候炎热、潮湿、多雨，因此传统的岭南建筑多在对自然环境的适应上，形成轻巧、开敞、通透的建筑风格，兼具通风、隔热、防晒、防潮等特点。外来建筑在进入岭南后也必须顺应气候特点，比如建筑间距离缩短，以减少人们在烈日下行走的时间。又如

陈家祠门廊 Portico of the Chen Clan Ancestral Hall

广州荔湾区恩宁路骑楼街
Arcade street on Enning Road of Liwan District of Guangzhou

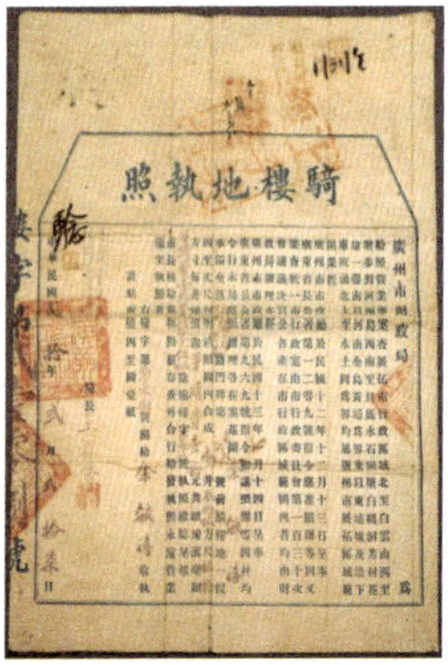

骑楼地执照，民国，广东省博物馆藏
Homestead License for the arcade (the Republic of China) • Guangdong Museum

SYMBIOSIS

The commercial culture in Lingnan region that is born with its long past and the constant inflow of foreign trading culture provides the foreign cultures with opportunities to exist and live on in Lingnan region. From the traditional buildings, temples, schools to modern arcades, shops, banks, schools, the styles of these buildings range from the academic style of Europe, and the modernist style to the traditional Chinese style, providing a mix of cultural symbiosis.

建筑使用大量通风设计，使用廊道来营造小气候环境，解决闷热潮湿的问题。建筑以实用为前提灵活多变。

多元共生

岭南地区长期以来形成的商业文化和对外贸易文化的持续输入，使外来文化在岭南地区占据一定地位，从传统建筑祠堂、书院，到近代建筑骑楼、商店、银行、学校，风格从欧洲学院派、现代主义，再到与中国元素折中等，形成不同文化间多元共生的态势。

东山小洋楼

Western-style building in Dongshan

HERITAGE AND REFORM

Due to the geographical distance from Central China, and the slow development in architectural scales and crafts, the crafts of Tang and Song dynasties can be seen in the buildings of Ming Dynasty in Guangzhou. Because of the differences in climate, material and usage, Lingnan architecture has underwent some changes while keeping its heritage. For example, the outside walls of some large buildings no longer use logs. Instead, stone pillars or high stone column bases or gables are used to resist humidity or termites for durability. Guangzhou residents also borrow the design of the quadrangle courtyard buildings in North China, but they change the design into that of "three houses with two corridors" to solve the problem of limited land with more people while the privacy of different houses is taken into consideration.

继承改良

由于与中原的地理相隔，建筑规模和工艺的传承缓慢，广州明代建筑中仍能找到唐宋工艺痕迹。但是由于气候、材料、用途等的不同，岭南建筑在继承中也做了改变。比如大型建筑的外圈弃用木头，改用石柱，或较高的石柱础，还有直接以山墙承重，这是为了防潮、防白蚁，更加耐用。又如广州民居吸收北方四合院的建筑理念，但根据平地少、人口密集的特点，又设计成各家相对独立，方便出入又便于联群的“三间两廊”基本格局。

“三间两廊”式房屋，位于广州黄埔区水西街

“Three-house-two-corridor” structure, Shuixi Street, Huangpu District, Guangzhou

DECORATIONS

The decoration for Lingnan buildings is characterized by its complicatedness. "The frequent rain in South China necessitates the special house ridges to avoid rain leakage, so the houses here often have big ridges which become a place to show the decoration crafts" (Chen Zehong, *The City Architecture in Guangzhou*). Besides, thanks to the long history of Lingnan region for its world trade, the city buildings in Guangzhou take in the technology and styles of the western architecture, which is something pioneering. The buildings in Hong Kong, Macao, Shisanhang, Shamian and the buildings of the western style provide visible references for architects.

LIME SCULPTURES

Lime sculptures use lime to make sculptures on the surface of the buildings. These sculptures are painted with

装饰美学

岭南建筑装饰细致精巧，“南方多雨，对屋脊构建的防漏功能有很高的要求，因此建造了特别粗大的屋脊，屋顶便成为了展示装饰工艺的理想之地”（陈泽泓《广州的城市建筑》）。此外，由于岭南地区长期的对外商贸交流，广州城市建筑在吸收西方建筑技术和风格的基础上，领风气之先。香港、澳门、十三行、沙面等地部分西方建筑的出现，为工匠提供直观的参考借鉴。

灰塑

灰塑，又称灰批，是指用石灰在建筑物上进行雕塑造型，再涂上绚丽色彩，线条粗放、层次分明，效果接近陶塑。在陈家祠和佛山祖庙均可见到清代灰塑作品。

灰塑《三福呈祥》
"Three Symbols of Bliss" (lime sculpture)

陈家祠屋顶上的陶塑、灰塑脊饰
Decorating pottery and lime sculptures on the ridges of the Chen Clan Ancestral Hall

bright colors which foreground their shapes and produce the effects of pottery. Lime sculptures which were common in Qing Dynasty can be seen in the Chen Clan Ancestral Hall and other family ancestral halls in Foshan.

POTTERY SCULPTURES

House ridges with pottery sculptures are also called "flower ridges". The pottery sculptures are made with clay which are then calcined, mainly used to decorate the ridges of large buildings. Pottery sculpture came to its prosperity in Qing Dynasty. There are altogether 11 flower ridges in the Chen Clan Ancestral Hall.

陶塑

陶塑脊饰，又称“花脊”，用陶泥雕塑后经煅烧而成，是专门装饰于大型建筑物屋脊的特殊工艺，清代在岭南最盛。陈家祠共有十一条陶塑脊饰。

陈家祠屋顶上的陶塑、灰塑脊饰
Decorating pottery and lime sculptures on the ridges of the Chen Clan Ancestral Hall

BRICK CARVINGS

Brick carvings can be divided into low carving, high carving and hollowed carving. The large-scale hollowed carving is favorable for heat releasing and ventilation.

WOOD CARVINGS

Wood carvings are mainly used to decorate the screens, partition boards, door canopies, angle braces, beam frames, and gable boards, featuring good ventilation and looking exquisite while allowing light into the rooms.

陈家祠的木雕
Wood carving of the Chen Clan Ancestral Hall

宝墨园入门砖雕

Tile Carving of the Gate at Baomo Garden

砖雕

技法有浅浮雕、高浮雕和透雕，大面积透雕的砖雕有利于建筑散热、透气、透风。

木雕

多用于屏风、隔扇子、门罩、挂落、梁架、封檐板，既通风采光，又呈现玲珑通透的意境。

广东一处四合院内的木雕

Wood carving in the quadrangle courtyard of Guangdong

STONE CARVINGS

To avoid the damage by damp-proof termites, the buildings in Lingnan region use stones to make breast boards, column bases, and beams on which are diversified beautiful carvings. Renwei Temple, the ornamental pillars before Nanhai Temple, the breast boards in the Chen Clan Ancestral Hall are representatives of stone carvings.

WESTERN DECORATIONS

黄埔公园
Huangpu Park

The flowered glass, blinds and the butterfly windows on the buildings near the Xiguan of Guangzhou and the arcades are classical western decorations. The first park in Guangzhou, Huangpu Park, was built by imitating the western parks. Its gate makes use of the three-arch Tuscan orders popular in ancient Rome. Guangdong Advisory Bureau of Guangzhou Government is housed in a group of buildings with both the Chinese and western architectural features. It imitates the parliament building of ancient Roman style, which reflects Guangzhou people's openness and their liking for what is beautiful.

石刻

为了防潮、防白蚁，岭南建筑的栏板、柱础、梁坊等多用石材，因此石刻造型饰样丰富。仁威庙、南海神庙华表、陈家祠栏板都是石刻艺术的代表作。

清朝石雕花件，广州南海神庙
Stone carving of Qing Dynasty • Nanhai Temple in Guangzhou

西饰

西关的骑楼装饰上，采用的蚀花玻璃、百叶窗、蝴蝶窗等，都是典型的西方建筑装饰。广州最早的公园是晚清所建的黄埔公园，仿建西方的园林建筑风格，大门是古罗马塔斯干柱式三拱西式。包括广州衙署建筑广东咨议局，也是中西合璧的建筑群，仿西方古罗马式议会大楼的形式，反映出岭南人开放融通、择善而从的特点。

广东咨议局 Guangdong Advisory Bureau

LOCAL TRADITION

ZHENHAI TOWER

Zhenhai Tower was first built in Ming Dynasty and underwent seven repairs. It has five stories, so it is also called "five-story tower". It is seated on top of minor Panlong Mound in Yuexiu District. It was originally built for military purpose, so its structure is different from the other towers in China that have doors on four sides. Three sides of this tower are walls with only window holes; on its southern side are corridors from which what is going on in the city can be seen. The other special places in Zhenhai Tower are that it looks like either a common building or a tower. The designer made use of the tower structure by which the four walls of the whole tower draw inside a little on each story while on each story the walls remain to be two meters in thickness. On the first and second stories, the walls are built with red sandstones which can bear great weight. When the walls on each story draw inside, the weight on top of the

地方
传统

镇海楼

始建于明代，历经七次大修。民间因其楼高五层，称其“五层楼”。位于越秀区小蟠龙岗上。由于镇海楼主要是军事用途，故结构不同于一般楼阁的四面通透，而是三面砌墙，只开窗洞，朝南一面阁状前出廊，方便俯瞰城内动向。镇海楼另一个特殊之处在于楼形如楼如塔，建造者利用塔式结构，山墙向上层层收缩，上下墙

镇海楼 Zhenhai Tower

walls is reduced, which provides Zhenhai Tower with a very stable structure.

THE CHEN CLAN ANCESTRAL HALL

There are a lot of temples in Guangzhou that were ever used as academies in the old days. Among them, the biggest one is the Chen Clan Ancestral Hall that was built during the reign of Emperor Guangxu in Qing Dynasty. It covers an area of more than 30,000 square meters and is the most intact, the most beautifully decorated ancient building. It is called the "Folk Art Museum of Guangdong". It is known for its "three carvings, three sculptures, and one iron cast".Three carvings refer to the stone lions in front of the gate, stone drums and the carvings on the stone pillars, the 6 groups of brick carvings that occupy 12 square meters, and the wood carvings on the beam frames, gable boards and the 12 teakwood partition doors. Three sculptures refer to the colored sculptures, clay sculptures and pottery sculptures on the ridges of the Chen Clan Ancestral Hall. One iron cast refers to the iron cast handicraft articles inside the temple. All are beautiful and gorgeous, embodying the superb crafts in Lingnan region.

BAMBOO TUBE HOUSE

The tube-like houses were the major form of buildings in Guangzhou in Ming and Qing dynasties. Such kind

厚度相差多达两米。底层、二层是极厚的红砂岩石墙体，承重能力强，上渐收缩又减轻上部压力，使镇海楼的结构稳定性远高于其他楼阁。

陈家祠

广州城内有许多以书院为形式的宗祠，其中建于清代光绪年间的陈家祠最大，占地面积3万多平方米，是广东现存规模最大、保存最完整、装饰最精美的古代艺术建筑，并成为广东民间工艺博物馆。著名的“三雕三塑一铸铁”的装饰艺术：“三雕”是指门口石狮、石鼓、石构柱础上的石雕，每幅12平方米、共6幅的砖雕，梁架、封檐板、聚贤堂内12扇柚木屏门等的木雕；“三塑”是指陈家祠房屋脊上的彩塑、灰塑和陶塑；“一铸”是指陈家祠内高超的铸铁工艺品，华丽繁复，展示了岭南工匠高超的装饰技艺。

陈家祠 The Chen Clan Ancestral Hall

广州西关竹筒屋的满洲窗
Manchuria style window of the bamboo-tube house in Xiguan of Guangzhou

of buildings solve the problem of limited space resulting from more and more prosperous commercial businesses in modern cities. The tube-like houses feature their narrow but long space, small but deep rooms. The facade of such kind of house usually amounts 3 to 4 meters, while the depth of its rooms is over 10 meters or more than 30 meters. Its rooms are arranged one by one from front to back, and the whole house looks like the tube of a piece of bamboo, so this kind of house is often called "bamboo-tube house". Bamboo-tube houses are narrow and deep, so the craftsmen designed skylights to divide the lobby and the private rooms, which solved the problem of ventilation, lighting and drainage.

XIGUAN MANSION

Xiguan Mansion is the representative of the large-

竹筒屋

明清时期广州城市居住主要建筑形式，是城市日益繁荣的商业发展带来的土地紧缺问题的解决方案。竹筒屋特点是布局狭长，单开间，开间小，进深大。门面大概只有三到四米，而进深长达十几米甚至三十米，由前到后排列成多个房间，状似竹筒，故被称为“竹筒屋”。由于竹筒屋面积狭窄，工匠们设计了天井分隔大厅和房间，以解决通风、采光和排水的问题。

广州的竹筒屋
Bamboo-tube house in Guangzhou

scale courtyard buildings in places around Guangzhou. They were the dwelling places of the big merchants or prestigious families. These buildings mainly gather near the Xiguan (west gate) of ancient Guangzhou and occupy very large space, so they are often termed as "Xiguan Mansion". The classical structure of this kind of buildings is that they have three houses, one in the middle and two with corridors on its right and left sides. The major house in the middle position is composed of the porch, foyer, lobby, first room, second lobby, second room; there are skylights to divide the lobbies; on top of the lobbies are side windows or top windows for lighting. The rooms on the right and left sides are used as libraries or minor lobbies. On the right and left sides of the major house are two narrow lanes that are used to control the temperature of the major house.

西关民俗馆，即西关大屋
Xiguan Folk Custom Museum (Xiguan Mansion)

There are three devices in the front gate of Xiguan Mansion: a foot door used for ventilation and to keep the owner's privacy as well; a gate bar made of logs that opens in horizontal direction, used for ventilation and safety of the people in the house; a big heavy door made of red sandalwood or the wood of Phoebe zhennan. The inside decoration of Xiguan Mansion is luxurious. There are trees, flowers, false hills, fish ponds in the courtyard, as well as exquisite wood carvings, stone carvings, brick carvings, and paintings, Manchu windows with Lingnan flavor. The owners of such buildings emphasize the different functions of the different devices while trying to provide a leisurely environment for their family members.

西关大屋传统民居客厅
Traditional Living Room of the folk building in Xiguan Mansion

西关大屋

岭南地区大型天井院落式住宅代表，为商业巨贾、名门望族居住。因主要集中在广州西关，房屋面积大，故被称为“西关大屋”。结构是典型的“三边过”，三间两廊，左右对称。中间为门廊、门厅、正厅、头房、二厅、二房，厅之间用小天井隔开，天井上有侧窗或天窗采光通风。两边是书房、偏厅等，大屋两侧还有两条通风降温的青云巷（冷巷）。

西关大屋正门有三件套：通风同时保持主人家私密的脚门，由圆木构成，横向开合；起通风和安保作用的趟栊；还有用红木或楠木制作的结实厚重的大门。西关大屋内设富丽堂皇，小院内栽花草，假山鱼池与厅房呼应，各类精致的木雕、石雕、砖雕、漆画等，以及富有岭南特色的满洲窗，都体现了主人既重功能又重享受的意识。

INCORPORATION OF FOREIGN ELEMENTS

ARCADES

Arcades are outer corridors of western style which are common in Hong Kong and Macao. They were built to fit the tropical or subtropical climate, and were favorable to be used for commercial purposes, so they were very common in Guangzhou. The arcades above the second story on the side that faces the street often stretch out over the street and are supported with pillars, while the inside parts are usually spacious spaces. The arcades of neighboring houses are often connected into one whole and form a sheltered passage for the pedestrians to fend off the sun and rain. Goods can also be displayed in the passage. Behind the arcades are storehouses; on top of them are dwelling places. This structure meets the needs of the commercial development for space, so that many buildings of such kind were constructed in the 1920s.

他山之石

骑楼

骑楼这种外廊式建筑最早在香港、澳门得到应用，因其适应热带、亚热带气候，且具备良好的商业用途，同处岭南的广州也迅速兴建骑楼。骑楼的沿街部分二层以上伸出街道，用立柱支撑，形成

广州北京路文化旅游区的骑楼建筑

Arcades in the Cultural Tourist District on Beijing Road of Guangzhou

SHISANHANG CHAMBER OF COMMERCE

After Guangzhou was open for world trade, the foreign merchants came to do businesses in Guangzhou, but they had to find the merchants Chinese government specified as their agencies and did businesses in specified places. This is the earliest form of Shisanhang (Thirteen Chamber of Commerce). It was roughly located in today's Culture Park, Shisanhang Street and South Renmin Road. The foreign merchants built their own assembly halls and houses according to the architectural style in their mother countries in the specified places. These buildings of the western style feature arched corridors, arched doors and windows, wall posts with chapiters and western gardens. Such kind of architectural style became very popular from that time on.

MERCHANT'S GARDENS

When they built their own gardens, the wealthy merchants made adaptations to the traditional Chinese gardens popular in Central and South China by adding corridors or cornices to cope with the hot and humid weather in Lingnan region while borrowing elements of the western architecture. The most famous one is Haishan Villa built by a rich merchant named Pan Shicheng. A French visitor wrote to his friend to describe this mercantile garden:

内部开敞空间。多户骑楼空间贯通，就形成了一条可以遮阳、避雨的人行通道，兼且可以进行商品展示。骑楼店铺后面为仓库，楼上住人，满足当时社会对商业发展的需求，故在20世纪20年代得到大量兴建。

十三行商馆

广州一口通商后，外商到广州进行贸易活动，必须找政府指定的行商作为代理，在划定的区域进行交易，这个区域就是十三行商馆，大概位于文化公园、十三行街、人民南路一带。外商在区域内按照自己国家的建筑风格修建商馆和住宅，西洋式的券廊、门窗券拱、西方流行的壁柱柱头，西式花园等随处可见。这些西方建筑处理手法也开始在岭南地区传播开来。

约1843年的纸上墨画，画中所描绘的是广州十三行商馆前景
Ink painting on paper (c. 1843, describing Shisanhang in Guangzhou)

1844年，广州荔湾的海山仙馆别墅，此别墅为清代广州富商潘仕成的宅邸，建于清道光年间
Haishan Villa in Liwan of Guangzhou in 1844 (the dwelling place of Pan Shicheng, a wealthy merchant in Guangzhou, built during the reign of Emperor Daoguang in Qing Dynasty)

"The floor is marble stones. Inside the house is marble stone pillars or sandalwood pillars decorated with pearls, gold, silver or emeralds…the furniture is covered with Japanese paint; velvet or silk carpets cover the floor of every room… the chandelier decorated with emeralds hang from the ceiling." This is the description of the architecture of that time with both Chinese and western elements.

行商园林

积累巨大财富的行商们在建造自家园林时，除了对中原、江南传统中式园林布局进行改良，增加廊、檐以适应高温高湿天气，在细节上也对西方建筑进行借鉴。最为出名的是行商潘仕成的别墅海山仙馆。有个法国人参观后，写信向朋友描述仙馆的西式奢华装修："地板是大理石的。房子里也装饰着大理石的圆柱，或者是镶嵌着珍珠母、金、银和宝石的檀木圆柱……家具漆着日本油漆，天鹅绒或丝质的地毯装点着一个个房间……镶着宝石的枝形吊灯从天花板上垂下来。"此充分说明当时中西合璧的建筑风格盛行。

1860年，广州的行商花园

A Merchant's garden in Guangzhou in 1860

INTEGRATED INNOVATION

SUN YAT-SEN MEMORIAL HALL

After the Opium War, the national consciousness among Chinese people became increasingly stronger. In terms of architecture, this national consciousness could be seen in Chinese people's exploration into the architectural styles peculiar to Chinese culture. Sun Yat-sen Memorial Hall is the representative of the peculiar Lingnan architecture. It takes the structure of Chinese palaces incorporating modern architectural technology. The outside is the two-dimensional octagonal structure imitating the royal palace in ancient China, looking quite majestic; the inside makes use of the western architectural materials—steel-reinforced concrete to build the pillars, floors and uses riveted steel beams to bear the weight of the roofs. While keeping the Chinese architectural elements, it uses modern architectural material and technology for the construction of a traditional Chinese building.

融合出新

中山纪念堂

鸦片战争以后，民族意识觉醒，反映在建筑上，便是第一次中国固有式建筑风格的探索与尝试。中山纪念堂的修建是岭南正式兴起固有式建筑风格的标志。它把仿宫殿式的风格和现代建筑技术相

20世纪30年代的广州中山纪念堂 Sun Yat-sen Memorial Hall in the 1930s

ARCHWAY OF SUN YAT-SEN UNIVERSITY

It was designed by two architects Yang Xizong and Lin Keming. The entrance archway was designed by Yang Xizong, which is a classical combination of Chinese stone archway and the triumphal arch in ancient Rome. The chemistry building of the Agriculture College and the teaching building of Department of Physics in School of Physics were designed by Lin Keming, which follows the peculiar Chinese architectural concepts, using diverse national crafts which stress economy, comfort and safety.

华南理工大学校门。此牌坊为中山大学石牌时期的老牌坊
Entrance Archway of South China University of Technology.This archway is the old one of Sun Yat-sen University in the period of Shipai

中山纪念堂
Sun Yat-sen Memorial Hall

结合，外部平面八角布局，为仿古宫殿式建筑，雄伟庄严；内部采用西方建筑材料钢筋混凝土建柱子、楼板，用铆接的钢屋架来负荷屋顶的全部重量。在保留中国韵味的同时，使用现代建筑材料和建筑技术来营造传统的中国建筑风格。

中山大学石牌校舍

中山大学石牌校舍由建筑师杨锡宗和林克明设计并修建。杨锡宗设计的入口牌坊，结合了中国的石牌坊和古罗马的凯旋门，是中西结合的经典。林克明设计农学院化学馆、理学院物理系教学楼等，贯穿“中国固有式建筑”理念，外形采用丰富多彩的民族传统手法，细节注重经济、舒适和安全。

ARCHITECTS

In the 1920s, many young students who studied in the universities of foreign countries returned home. Many of them who studied architecture were Cantonese people. The 8 departments of architecture established during the Republic of China were opened by 6 Lingnan architects, including Lin Keming who established Department of Architecture in Xiangqin University in 1932. Yang Xizong, Xia Changshi, Chen Boqi, Lin Keming and some others designed the buildings such as Beiyuan Restaurant, the Canton Fair, the Exihibition Hall of South China Local Specialty. This is their contribution to the diversity of Guangzhou architecture in the 20th century.

LIN KEMING:REPRESENTATIVE OF MODERNISM

Born in Dongguan of Guangdong Province, Lin Keming (1900–1999) graduated from the Department of Civil Engineering of Lyon School of Architecture and Engineering. Lin actively joined the exploration of designing architectures with "China's intrinsic characteristics", and later successively completed the design of some large-scale public buildings such as the Sun Yat-Sen Library, the Guangzhou Municipal Government Office Building, and the New School Buildings of Sun Yat-sen University at Shipai, Guangzhou.

名师
风范

20世纪20年代，大批留学生学成归国，学建筑的广东人占了很高的比例。创办于民国时期的8个大学建筑系，是由6位广东籍建筑师所创办的，包括1932年林克明在广州创办的勷勤大学建筑系。杨锡宗、夏昌世、陈伯齐、林克明等设计了一批如北园酒家、广交会、华南土特产展览交流大会等现代建筑，为20世纪岭南建筑的丰富多彩作出巨大贡献。

林克明
Lin Keming

林克明：现代主义

林克明（1900—1999），广东东莞人，法国里昂建筑工程学院建筑学系毕业。林克明主动加入了“中国固有式”建筑的探索，

XIA CHANGSHI: ARCHITECTURE TO SERVE MAN

Born in Guangzhou, Xia Changshi (1903–1996) graduated from the University of Karlsruhe in Germany, and in 1945 he was invited to work in Department of Civil Engineering at Sun Yat-Sen University. He emphasized that architecture must serve the need of man and the fundamental importance of architecture was to create a healthy and comfortable living environment for human. In 1951, the Exposition of Lingnan Local Products designed by him was completed and was praised as “a pioneer of modern Lingnan architecture” .

MO BOZHI： INCLUSIVENESS & VANGUARD

Born in Dongguan of Guangdong Province, Mo Bozhi (1914–2003) graduated from the Department of Civil Engineering of the Engineering School of Sun Yat-sen University in Guangzhou. He began his career by exploring and practicing the combination of the characteristics of Lingnan garden and the modern architectures, and in the early stage his representative works were 3 garden restaurants, namely Beiyuan Restaurant, Panxi Restaurant and Nanyuan Restaurant. And in his later stage of architectural design, he still adhered to the practice of combining garden and architecture, and his master works were New Aiqun Hotel, Guangzhou Hotel， Baiyun Hotel and the White Swan Hotel.

Adviser of this Chapter: Chen Zehong (Academic member of the Committee of Chinese local chronicles, Director and the Research Institute of the Academic Committee of Literature and History, Guangzhou Municipal People's Government)

先后完成了中山图书馆、广州市府合署、中山大学石牌新校舍等大型公共建筑设计。

夏昌世：为“人”服务

夏昌世（1903—1996），广东新会人，毕业于德国卡尔斯鲁厄工业大学建筑专业。1945年应邀到中山大学建筑系任教。夏昌世强调建筑是为“人”服务的，以创造健康舒适的人居环境为第一要义。1951年，夏昌世创作了华南土特产展览交流大会，该作品被称为“当代岭南建筑的先声”。

夏昌世
Xia Changshi

莫伯治：包容与超前

莫伯治（1914—2003），广东东莞人，毕业于广州中山大学工程院土木建筑系。以北园、泮溪、南园三个园林酒家为开端探索岭南庭园与现代建筑融合的探索实践，后期创作新爱群大厦、广州宾馆、白云宾馆和白天鹅宾馆依旧坚持庭园与建筑的结合实践。

莫伯治
Mo Bozhi

本章顾问：陈泽泓（中国地方志学会学术委员，广州市人民政府文史研究馆文史学术委员会主任、历史学研究员）

PREVAILING CUSTOM
—LINGNAN CUSTOMS

Lingnan culture is open, diversified and inclusive, practical and innovative, producing very special regional folk arts and customs. A large group of precious traditional crafts and fine arts are well preserved in Guangzhou, including jade carvings, wood carvings, tusk carvings, Cantonese color pottery, Cantonese embroidery. Flower fair, dragon boat race and Cantonese lion dance are the old customs that are still very popular today in Guangzhou. They are the name cards of Lingnan, presenting to the world an old, colorful and vivid culture.

风尚

岭南民俗

岭南文化开放、多元、包容、务实和创新的精神气质，孕育出极富地域文化特色的岭南民间工艺和节俗风貌。广州目前保存了一大批弥足珍贵的传统工艺美术项目，其中玉雕、木雕、牙雕、广彩、广绣等传统工艺精绝卓著。广州至今仍保留着行花街、龙舟竞渡、醒狮等古老的节俗，作为岭南的特色名片，向世界展示积淀深厚、多元鲜活的岭南文化特色。

CULTURAL ROOT

HISTORY

The archaeological discoveries of potteries and bones with geometric images prove that the folk arts and crafts in Lingnan region can be traced to the days of the ancient Nanyue Kingdom.

The favorable geological environment, the exclusive status as a world trading port, the congregation of Chinese and western cultures, thoughts, technologies and crafts in Guangzhou since Ming and Qing dynasties made it possible for the commercial activities and handicrafts here to continuc to prosper for over a thousand years. Lingnan arts and crafts never gave up its traditions while making innovations and changes to combine both the east and the west, which produced exhilarating crafts peculiar to Lingnan region.

The tusk carvings, jade carvings, wood carvings, colored Cantonese potteries and Cantonese embroideries

寻根溯源

源远流长

几何印纹陶器、骨器等现代考古的发现，证实了岭南民间工艺的历史可上溯至远古南越族时代。

明清至近代以来，优越的地缘环境，“一口通商”政策的实施，中西文化、思潮、科技、工艺的汇聚交融，使广州千年的商贸

南越王宫博物馆

Nanyue Kingdom Palace Museum

feature diverse artistic topics and exquisite shapes by combining Chinese and the western cultures and arts. Therefore, these traditional crafts treasured by the local people and the world embody the peculiar glamour of Lingnan culture.

INCLUSIVENESS AND DIVERSITY

Since Qin and Han dynasties, while trading frequently with the world across the sea, the people of Guangzhou have been making efforts to combine the cultures of Central China and those from the vast world with the local cultures to form a diversified culture. Lingnan customs are also the miniature of the cultural communication between the south and the north, between China and the West.

Lingnan customs are peculiar for their special features, lively and pleasant, overflowing with the romantic tone of Lingnan water regions and the city of flowers. These customs include the flower fair on the eve of the Lunar New Year, the dragon boat race during the Dragon Boat Festival, the lion dance during various ceremonies, and Piaose to worship gods as well. These customs enbody rich cultural meanings for the local people to beg for a good year, to celebrate the good harvest, to worship gods or to entertain themselves. They have a history of thousands of years, but are still full of vitality.

昌盛和繁荣的手工业得以延续。岭南工艺在继承传统的同时，又应市场需求不断创新求变，不拘一格、中西合璧，最终发展出令人惊叹的技艺，形成了富于岭南特色的独特风格。

牙雕、玉雕、木雕、广彩、广绣等传统广式工艺，取材多样、造型精美，融合了中西文化和艺术审美，成为备受时人推崇的奇珍神作，并风行世界，彰显岭南文化的独特魅力。

兼容多姿

自秦汉以来，岭南百越先民在频繁的海上贸易往来中，不断将中原文化和海外文化融入本土文化，形成多元包容的文化特色。岭南节俗也处处显露出南北交融、中西荟萃的特色。

岭南民间游艺个性鲜明、活泼明快，充满岭南水乡和鲜花之城的浪漫情调，如除夕行花街、端午扒龙舟、节庆舞醒狮、迎神飘色游艺等。这些别具一格的民间游艺，蕴含了祈年、庆丰、祝颂、娱乐等朴素多样的文化内涵，传承千年，历久弥新。

越秀西湖花市上的醒狮表演

The lion dance during Xihu Flower Fair of Yuexiu District

CANTONESE TREASURES

CANTONESE PORCELAIN

"Golden threads weave the white jade, and Spring flowers bloom on silvery porcelain." This poetic line describes the beauty of colored Cantonese potteries. Colored Cantonese porcelain is the short form of "colored Cantonese porcelain with golden lines". It first came out during the reign of Emperor Kangxi in Qing Dynasty, a kind of overglazed colored porcelain designed mainly to export to other countries. It is one of the three kinds of potteries designed for exportation that enjoys the reputation of "exquisite crafts as precious as gold and jade". By now, it has a history of 300 years.

The period from Emperor Kangxi to Emperor Yongzheng was the early stage in the history of colored Cantonese porcelain. At that time, the western crafts of "glazing over metallic surface" spread to Guangzhou. The craftsmen in Guangzhou invented glazing over copper

广彩：绚丽华彩

“万缕金丝织白玉，春花飞上银瓷面”，这著名的诗句说的正是广彩。广彩是“广州织金彩瓷”的简称，始于清代康熙时期，是专门为外销而生产的釉上彩绘瓷器品种，是中国三大外销瓷器之一，有“工细殊绝，堆金积玉”的美誉，至今已有三百年历史。

清乾隆广彩人物故事图折沿碟
Edge-folded Cantonese colored porcelain tray made in Qing Dynasty with pictures of human figures

surface and then they moved this craft to white porcelain surface. That was the overglazed porcelain, the early form of colored Cantonese porcelain.

During the reign of Emperor Qianlong, the market of colored Cantonese porcelain spread from Europe to the United States. Patterns with golden lines began to be used on the porcelain, and the major colors used were turquoise blue, bright red, bright green, eggplant purple and golden, which made the colored patterns on the porcelain look like golden threads zigzagging on the white jade, so this kind of porcelain were also called "golden-lined colored porcelain". Its bright colors, exquisite patterns, delicate delineation became the peculiar symbols of colored Cantonese porcelain, and this tradition is still observed today.

At the turn of the 19th and 20th century, the forerunners of Lingnan painting, Gao Jianfu and Chen Shuren, participated in the technological studies and practices of colored Cantonese porcelain, which helped colored Cantonese porcelain gain a new life. Since the founding of the People's Republic of China, while inheriting the tradition, the craftsmen of colored Cantonese porcelain were always trying new things for its diversity and innovation. In 2008, colored Cantonese porcelain was listed among the second group of national intangible cultural heritages. Colored Cantonese porcelain has come to a new stage in its history.

清嘉庆广彩绘人物圆形瓷板，广州博物馆藏
Round Cantonese color porcelain plate with pictures of human figures made during the Reign of Emperor Jiaqing in Qing Dynasty • Guangzhou Museum

康熙到雍正时期是广彩的初创阶段。当时西方“金胎烧珐琅”技法传到广州，广州工匠创制出“铜胎烧珐琅”，后把这种方法用在白瓷胎上，成为珐琅彩，是广彩的萌芽。

乾隆年间，广彩的销售市场逐步从欧洲转向以美国为主，广彩开始大量采用织金图案的手法，以水青、大红、大绿、茄紫、金彩等色彩为主，犹如万缕金丝织白玉，因此又被称为“织金彩瓷”。这种色彩艳丽、构图严谨、绘工精细、金碧耀眼的风格，成为广彩独树一帜的典型特色，并延续至今。

19世纪末20世纪初，岭南画派开创者高剑父、陈树人等积极参与广彩的技术研究和实践，为广彩技艺注入新的生机。新中国成立至今，在继承传统的同时，广彩工匠走上多元化及变革之路。2008年广彩被列入第二批国家非物质文化遗产名录，广彩发展迎来新的辉煌。

GOLDEN CANTONESE EMBROIDERY

Guangzhou embroidery refers to the embroidery of Guangzhou, one of the four famous embroideries in China. Cantonese embroidery also includes Chaozhou embroidery. Since Tang Dynasty, Guangzhou embroidery had been known for its superb crafts. It is believed that Lu Meiniang from Nanhai was summoned to serve the royal court because of her superb embroidery crafts. In Ming and Qing dynasties, Guangzhou embroidery was sent to the royal court as tributes. Besides it was also used in daily life.

Over its long history, Guangzhou embroidery enjoyed a good reputation at home and abroad for its super crafts, varieties, exquisite patterns, bright colors and exotic decorative effects. It has a glorious past like that of Lingnan painting and Lingnan opera. In 1929, an embroidery exposition was held in Guangzhou. Guangzhou embroidery provided such representative works as "Peacocks and Peony", "Lions" and "The Snow Landscape" which won the praise of the audience.

晚清广绣《三羊开泰图》
"Three Goats Bringing Bliss" (Cantonese embroidery in the late of Qing Dynasty)

After the founding of the People's Republic of China, Guangzhou embroidery experienced various innovations. There appeared such new products as pearl embroidery, tapestry and drawnwork. Guangzhou embroidery master Chen Shaofang innovatively put the essence of Chinese and the western paintings and formative arts into Guangzhou embroidery to invent the peculiar Chens' Guangzhou embroidery which was passed over to the later generation

民国广绣缠枝莲纹汉褂
Han clothing with embroidered lotus and spiral sprays made in the Republic of China

广绣：金丝锦绣

广绣是广州刺绣的简称，与潮州刺绣合称粤绣，被誉为中国“四大名绣”之一。从唐代开始广绣已经有相当高超的技艺，相传南海卢眉娘以刺绣工艺精巧被传入宫中刺绣。明清时期，广绣被当作贡品进献宫廷，广绣日用品也被广泛应用于日常生活中。

长久以来，广绣以其艺术精湛、品种繁多、技法多变、构图饱满、色调瑰丽、装饰性强等独特风格享誉海内外。其发展历程与岭南画派、岭南戏曲等文化艺术相辅相成。1929年，广州举办绣品展览赛，广绣参展作品《孔雀牡丹》《番狮》《雪地风景》等大获赞誉。

新中国成立后，广绣获得创新性传承发展，出现织锦等新兴产品。广绣大师陈少芳创造性地将中西绘画造型艺术的精髓注入传统广绣中，独创“陈氏广绣”，并传承给后代，获得世人认可。2006年，

and won a fame all over the world. In 2006, Guangzhou embroidery was listed among the first group of national intangible cultural heritages; in 2018 it was listed among the first group of national traditional crafts needed to be revived, which gave this kind of folk crafts a new life.

PRECIOUS CANTONESE JADE CARVINGS

广州玉雕《岫玉云龙球》
"Jade Ball with Cloud and Dragon" (Cantonese Jade Carving)

Cantonese jade carving is the traditional folk crafts that makes carvings on jades. It is known for its elegance, delicateness, exquisiteness and rich varieties. It occupies the handicraft market with its hollowed-out brackets, hollow-engraved jade balls and composite embeddings. It features the essence of Lingnan culture and is regarded as one of the four kinds of jade carvings in China.

The history of Cantonese jade carving can be traced back to the days in the ancient Nanyue Kingdom 2000 years ago. The jade clothing found in the tomb of Nanyue King in Han Dynasty indicated that Cantonese jade carving was already known for its superb crafts at that time. The record of Cantonese jade carving began in Tang Dynasty. In the years of the Republic of China, Cantonese jade carving reached its peak, represented by the jade markets dug out near Changshou Road and Daihe Road. The jewelries produced at that time topped the whole country.

After the founding of the People's Republic of China, Cantonese jade carving witnessed its second renaissance.

广绣被列入第一批国家级非遗代表性项目名录，2018年被列入第一批国家传统工艺振兴目录，在新时代焕发新的生机。

广州玉雕：华贵精绝

广州玉雕是以翡翠玉为原材料进行雕刻的传统民间手工技艺，以典雅秀丽、玲珑剔透、雕法细腻、品种繁多见长，以通雕座件、镂雕玉球、组合镶嵌等工艺技法独步业界，独具岭南文化内蕴特色，被公认为中国玉雕四大派之一。

广州玉雕的历史可追溯到两千多年前的古南越国时期，西汉南越王墓出土的丝缕玉衣，显示当时广州玉雕已有高超技艺。有历史记载的广州玉雕工艺始于唐代。民国时，广州玉器业进入全

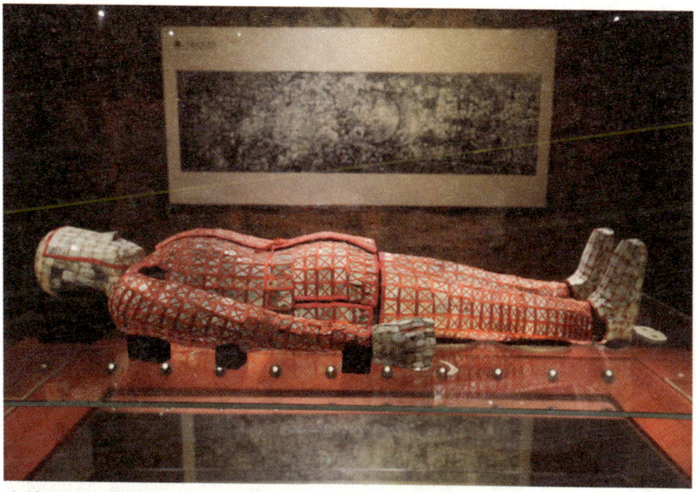

南越王赵眜的丝缕玉衣，广州西汉南越王博物馆藏
Jade Clothing of Zhao Mo, Nanyue King • Nanyue King Tomb Museum of West Han Dynasty in Guangzhou

Towards the end of the 1980s, a lot of jade carving masters gathered in South China Jade Carving Factory. The multi-layered hollow-engraved jade balls are the most precious product of Cantonese carving, featuring peculiar carving techniques, smoothing sliding devices, beautiful surface carvings of birds, flowers, dragon and phoenixes, and winning a good reputation all over the world.

CANTONESE WOOD CARVINGS INCORPORATING THE EASTERN AND THE WESTERN CRAFTS

Cantonese wood carving is a special one among the wood carvings in China. It is made mainly on hard wood such as red sandalwood, santos rosewood and rosewood, used mainly to decorate furniture, screens, palace lanterns, brackets or as architectural particles. The craft to make Cantonese hard-wood furniture is the most important representative folk craft of Guangzhou, whose history can be traced back to the time at the turn of Ming and Qing dynasties. It has a history of over 300 years, often termed as "Cantonese wood furniture", one of the 3 kinds of famous furniture in China.

Cantonese furniture is usually made of thick log wood, featuring its thick boards and luxurious decoration. It absorbs many exotic decorative crafts followed by other folk arts, especially known for pattern carving and embedding crafts. The complicated decoration, broad and deep carving,

广州玉雕《翡翠指溢金元》
"Jade Fingers Holding Coins"
(Cantonese Jade Carving)

盛时期，以长寿路和带河路的玉器墟最为繁荣，广州生产的珠宝饰品冠绝全国。

新中国成立后，广州玉雕再度兴盛。20世纪80年代末，南方玉雕厂聚集了众多顶尖的玉雕艺人。其中，镂雕多层玉球是广州玉雕的精品，创新独特技法，玉球层层重叠，转动自如，表层雕刻精美花鸟、龙凤等，工艺精绝，享誉国际。

广式木雕：中西合璧

在中国流派众多的木雕艺术中，广式木雕独树一帜，它多指对紫檀、酸枝、花梨等硬木材料的雕刻，主要用于家具、屏风、宫灯、座件、建筑饰件等。其中的广式硬木家具制作技艺是广州民间传统手工技艺的重要代表，其历史可追溯到明末清初，至今已有300多年，世称"广木作"，是我国家具三大流派之一。

广式木作家具取材粗大、造型厚重、装饰华丽，在工艺上吸收

and exquisite polishing give Cantonese furniture luxurious flavor. Cantonese furniture never stops absorbing and integrating the western cultural elements, vividly illustrating the open, innovative nature of Lingnan culture. After the founding of the People's Republic of China, the craftsmen of Cantonese wood carving continued to make innovations while keeping the excellent traditions to produce exquisite products. The 10-head bed with ding-pattern carvings, the 10-head bed with dragon-pattern carvings, and the 7-head round table with plum-flower and bird-pattern carvings were exhibited in National Exposition of Handicrafts and Fine Arts and won the praise of the people. In 2018, it was listed in the Plan on Revitalizing China's Traditional Crafts.

EXQUISITELY CARVED CANTONESE TUSK CARVINGS

Cantonese tusk carving is also called the "southern tusk carving". It uses elephant tusks as the material to make carvings. This traditional folk handicraft has a long history that can be traced back to Han and Tang dynasties, and it prospered in Ming and Qing dynasties. At the turn of Qing Dynasty and the Republic of China, there occurred a whole street where tusk carvings were selling. In modern China, Cantonese tusk carving became one of the three important tusk carvings in China with its peculiar Lingnan flavor. The representative products are hollow-engraved tusk balls,

了众多瑰丽的装饰手法，尤以雕花装饰和镶嵌工艺见长。繁复的装饰、宽深的雕刻、精细的磨工，使广式家具呈现豪华富丽的风格特色。广式家具不断吸纳、融合西洋文化，是早期“中西合璧”的成功诠释，充分显现岭南文化开放创新、兼容并蓄的特色。新中国成立后，广州木雕艺人在传承传统的同时，大胆创新设计观念，家具精品迭出。“宝鼎十头床”“龙十头床”“梅雀七头大圆台”等广式家具参加全国工艺美术展并大获好评。2018年广州木雕入选第一批国家传统工艺振兴目录。

广州牙雕：精雕细镂

广州牙雕又称“南派牙雕”，是以象牙为原材料进行雕刻的传统民间手工技艺，历史悠久，起于汉唐，盛于明清。清末民初，广

牙雕《羊城八景》 “Eight Scenes of Guangzhou” (tusk carving)

miniature boats, mini paintings.

Cantonese tusk carving is known for its exquisite carving techniques. The exquisite hollow engraving is what makes it so special. During the reign of Emperor Qianlong, the craftsmen of Cantonese tusk carving could create 11-layered tusk balls. In 1915, the 25-layered tusk balls created by Cantonese tusk carving craftsmen Weng Zhao and Liang Xiong won the award in that year's World's Fair, which won Chinese tusk carving a good fame.

牙雕《敦煌梦》
"Dreaming Dunhuang"
(tusk carving)

After the founding of the People's Republic of China, Cantonese tusk carving witnessed the rapid growth in world trade. In the 1980s, the world trade of Cantonese tusk carvings came to its prosperous stage: carved tusk balls, mini tusk ships carved with dragons and phoenixes won many awards. In 2006, Cantonese tusk carving was listed among the first group of national intangible cultural heritages.

“鬼工球”即套球，又称“同心球”，是广州最有代表性的牙雕制品
Concentric ball (the representative tusk carving of Guangzhou)

州出现成行成市的大新象牙街。近代以来，广州牙雕以其独具岭南特色的风格，成为中国三大牙雕流派之一，以镂雕牙球、画舫、微刻书画等为代表。

广州牙雕以玲珑剔透、精雕细镂的技法闻名，独特的镂空、透深的雕刻技法是其巧夺天工的精妙所在。乾隆时期，广州牙雕已能精雕细镂11层象牙球。1915年，广州牙雕艺人翁昭、梁雄创作的25层象牙球获得万国博览会优胜奖，使中国牙雕名满天下。

新中国成立后，广州牙雕工艺品进出口贸易兴旺，20世纪80年代进入最繁荣时期，象牙球、象牙龙凤船等大批南派牙雕代表作品多次获奖。2006年广州牙雕被列入中国首批非物质文化遗产保护名录。

COLORFUL FESTIVALS

FLOWER FAIR TO WELCOME THE NEW YEAR

Guangzhou is also called the "City of Flowers". The mild climate and fertile land cultivate the industry of flower planting and appreciation whose history can be traced back to the years of Qin and Han dynasties 2000 years ago. By Ming and Qing dynasties, with the increase in economic power and population, flower consumption became one of the major industries in Guangzhou.

The prosperous flower trade cultivates the custom among Cantonese people to plant flowers, buy flowers or appreciate flowers. The most important is that it creates the tradition of Flower Fair to celebrate the coming of the lunar new year. In the later part of Qing Dynasty, Guangzhou was the first to begin the Flower Fair. The Flower Fair at that time was celebrated in the district around Shuangmendi (today's Beijing Road) in Guangzhou City. Visiting the Flower Fair became gradually a local custom. The Flower

多彩
节俗

迎春花市：行花街

广州素有“花城”美誉，气候温润、物产丰盛，种花养花为业、赏花爱花成俗的历史，可以追溯到两千年前的秦汉时期。至明清，随着经济繁盛和人口增加，花卉种植业飞跃而成广州重要的经济产业之一。

广州市民行花街

Guangzhou People go to the Flower Fair

Fair is held today three days before the New Year's Eve. According to the record in *The Chronicle of Guangzhou City*, the Flower Fair in Guangzhou City is gorgeous, with a sea of flowers and waves after waves of visitors.

Since the opening-up policy was launched, the Flower Fair thrives year by year. In the recent years, "visiting the Flower Fair to spend the Spring Festival in Guangzhou" became the most important custom of Guangzhou and the name card of Guangzhou as well, which has promoted the profile of Guangzhou in the age of cultural globalization.

DRAGON BOAT RACE

From April to June each year, Lingnan region enters the rainy season, which is often called "dragon boat rain". This suggests that it is the right season for the dragon boat race. The race can be seen on Pearl River, Lizhi Bay, Huadi River, Chebei River... In Guangzhou, wherever there is water, the dragon boats can be seen. On the day of Dragon Boast Festival (the fifth day of the lunar May), the dragon boat race is on everywhere where thousands of people gather.

The rivers zigzag across Pearl River Delta which takes Guangzhou as the center. The people of the ancient Nanyue Kingdom took the boats as their homes, took the dragon as their totem, and chose to row the dragon boat to celebrate the dragon and to entertain themselves. With

繁荣的花市贸易滋养出广州人爱种花、爱买花、爱赏花的诗意风俗，还催生了最重要的广州年俗——迎春花市。清中叶后，广州在全国首创迎春花市，当时花市设在广州城内双门底（今北京路）一带。民国时期，游花市逐渐成为广州习俗，每年花市在除夕前三天举行。据《广州城坊志》所记的花市盛况："每逢除夕之夜，广州城的花市蔚为壮观，鲜花十里，人海如潮。"

改革开放后，迎春花市更添兴盛。近年，"广州过年，花城看花"成为越来越具影响力的新年俗和广州城市文化名片，持续提升广州的全球文化影响力。

龙舟盛景：趁景斗标

每年4至6月，岭南地区雨季来临，俗称"龙舟水"，就到了"扒龙舟"的好时节。珠江、荔枝湾、花地河、车陂涌……在广

清末的广州，盛大的赛龙舟活动正在举行

Scene of the ongoing dragon boat race in late Qing Dynasty in Guangzhou

the time passing by, the Dragon Boat Festival was given new historical meanings. It has become a festival that connects the people from both the south and the north. And the ceremonious dragon boat race has already become the traditional custom of Guangzhou. In Song Dynasty, there was already large-scale dragon boat race in Guangzhou. In Ming and Qing dynasties, there were many records about the race during the Dragon Boat Festival. Qu Dajun, a scholar living in the Late Ming dynasty, once gave a detailed description of the race in Pearl River Delta during the Dragon Boat Festival in his book *A New Brief Sketch of Guangdong*.

From the beginning to the end, the dragon boat race in Guangzhou every year will last over a month. From this festival, there comes many other customs with rich local color, such as "dragon boat meal" and "dragon boat bath" which have become special parts of the dragon boat culture.

The core of the dragon boat race is the dragon boat performances and the race. The dragon boat performance means that every year during the Dragon Boat Festival, the dragon boats from different places gather together to do various performances and the people will gather to enjoy the festival. The performances may be done in different places. The race refers to the dragon boat race where the people row their dragon boats for competition on the water. As the saying goes, "good race, good life."

In 1994, the municipal government of Guangzhou officially set the day of the Dragon Boat Festival as the

州，有水的地方就有龙舟的身影。农历五月初五端午节那天，龙舟竞渡，万众观赏，是岭南地区的一大盛景。

以广州为中心的珠三角地区河网密布，古越人以舟楫为家，以龙为图腾，他们选择在端午节划龙舟祭龙，娱神自娱。世更时移，端午被赋予更多历史内涵，成为南北融合的风俗节日，充满仪式感的龙舟盛景也成为岭南人特有的传统民俗。南宋广州民间已有大型的龙舟竞渡。明清时期，关于广州端午节赛龙舟的盛况已有详细的记载，如屈大均在《广东新语》中曾经描述过珠三角端午节期间的赛龙夺锦场面。

从“起龙”“采青”“趁景”到最后的“藏龙”，每年广州的龙舟盛事往往要历时一个多月，由此还衍生出许多富有地方特色的风俗，比如“食龙船饭”“洗龙舟水”等，已然成为一种独特的龙舟文化。

龙舟竞渡 Dragon boat race

day to hold the boat race. In 2010, the dragon boat race for the first time became a competition event in the Asian Games. And in 2011, the dragon boat was list among the city intangible cultural heritages of Guangzhou. Today, during the Dragon Boat Festival every year, various kinds of dragon boats move about on the waters of Guangzhou, turning this old tradition into one event with life.

COLORFUL SHAWAN PIAOSE

The old saying goes, "Lunar March 3, the birthday of Northern God is the day you come to Shawan to enjoy Piaose." Piaose is a traditional folk event with conspicuous local color. It developed from the event to celebrate the gods represented by Northern God. Its long history, the beautiful board figures, the various colors and the superb performing skills turned Shawan piaose into the representative of this kind of customs of Guangdong province.

It is recorded that there already had Shawan Piaose at as late as the turn of Ming and Qing dynasties. The traditional Shawan Piaose is done on the third day of the lunar March each year to celebrate the birthday of Northern God. Shawan is located in the water region. In the past, there were often floods. In order to fend off the floods, the people of Shawan hoped to protect themselves by worshiping the god of water, Northern God. On the birthday of Northern God, the local people will use a specially made

扒龙舟的核心主要有趁景、斗标两种形式。所谓趁景，又称“龙船景”，是指端午期间，各方龙船前来应景，聚集一起表演扒龙舟、走亲会友，轮流在各乡举行。斗标则是“斗龙船”，也即著名的“赛龙夺锦”。正如人们的美好愿景：“龙舟扒得快，今年好世界。”

1994年，广州市人民政府正式把端午节定为龙舟节。2010年龙舟首次成为亚运会比赛项目。2011年，龙舟入选广州市非遗目录。如今，每到端午时节，多种多样的龙舟节庆十分活跃，显示了这一古老节俗鲜活的现代传承。

沙湾飘色：“色”艺俱佳

“三月三，北帝诞，睇飘色，嚟沙湾”，这句俗谚说的正是沙湾飘色。这是一项具有沙湾本土文化特色的传统民间艺术活动，由

广州番禺沙湾飘色《赛龙夺锦》
“Dragon Boat Race Champion” (Shawan Piaose at Panyu of Guangzhou)

steel rod with a board on top to raise the child protagonists in the air during the parade. The parade is a grandeur. By this, the local people hope to beg a peaceful new year.

The traditional Shawan Piaose consists of the board on the bottom (called se gui in Chinese), 8 to 10 years old children in ancient costume on top of the board (called ping in Chinese), about 2-year-old children on top of ping (called piao) and the invisible rod supporting the children (called se geng). The four parts combine into one whole by which the parade tells stories of a whole set of figures.

The Shawan Piaose is a special kind of folk art that combines opera, music, dance, clothing, make-up, acrobatics, sculptures, folk crafts and fine arts into one, characterized by its rich cultural connotations, special forms, superb skills and bright colors. Its formation, costumes, and performances all incorporate the artistic elements of Cantonese opera, Cantonese music, Cantonese embroidery and lion dance, featuring peculiar Lingnan culture. In 2000, Shawan was named by the Ministry of Culture as the "hometown of Chinese folk art (floral board parade)".

LION DANCE OF POWER AND BEAUTY

Lion dance is one of the traditional folk art in China, which has a long history. The lion dance in China is often classified as the "southern lion" and the "northern lion". The "southern lion" is seen in Lingnan region, sometimes called

沙湾北帝诞迎神赛会娱神节目发展而来。以悠久的历史、丰富的板色、艳丽的色彩和高超的技艺闻名于世，成为广东飘色的代表。

据史载，最迟在明末清初沙湾已经有飘色。传统的沙湾飘色巡游在每年农历三月初三北帝诞举行。沙湾地处水乡，古时常有水患，为了免遭水患，沙湾人希望通过供奉水神北帝获得保佑。在北帝诞这一天，以一根特别的钢筋使扮演故事主角的孩童凌空飘起，声势浩大地穿街过巷巡游，祈求风调雨顺、吉祥如意。

传统的沙湾飘色由色柜、“屏”、“飘”和色梗组成，四者巧妙连接起来组成一板完整飘色，塑造一组人物或故事情景。

沙湾飘色是融合了戏剧、音乐、舞蹈、服饰、化妆、杂技、雕塑以及工艺美术为一体的综合民间艺术，底蕴丰富、造型独特、技艺精湛、色彩艳丽。从制作、装扮到表演，都体现了对粤剧、广东音乐、广绣、龙狮舞等岭南民间文艺的吸收与融合，具有浓郁的岭南文化特色。2000年，沙湾镇被文化部命名为“中国民间（飘色）艺术之乡”。

醒狮献瑞：力美融合

舞狮是我国具有悠久历史和民族特色的传统民间游艺，历来有“北狮”和“南狮”两大流派。南狮主要流行于岭南一带，又称“醒狮”。

五代十国后，随着中原移民的南迁，舞狮文化传入岭南地区，醒狮由唐代宫廷狮子舞脱胎而来。醒狮被认为是驱邪避害的吉祥瑞物，每逢节庆或重大活动，必有醒狮助兴，后逐渐形成独具岭南地

the "waking lion".

After the period of five dynasties and ten kingdoms period A.D. 907–979 came to the end, with more and more people from Central China moved south, the lion dance was also brought to Lingnan region. The southern lion dance developed from the lion dance in the royal court of Tang Dynasty. The lion dance in Lingnan region is regarded as the event to drive away harmful forces. The lion dance is performed whenever there is celebration ceremonies or other important events. It has become an event peculiar to Lingnan region that has passed on or will be passed on for generations.

The key to the lion dance is its "waking" state. The shape of the lion is peculiar to Lingnan region, looking powerful and vivid with scales all over its body. The head of the lion is exquisitely made, making the lion look like a real one. The intermingled black and white, or red and green make it easy to attract the attention of the audience. All the decorations on the lion make it look very powerful like the real king of animals. According to their shapes, the lions can be divided into "wen lions", "wu lions", "color lions", "black-white lions" and many other varieties. With the lion dance becoming more and more popular, beginning in Ming and Qing dynasties, the decoration of the lion's head became an industry peculiar to Lingnan region.

The lion dance needs skills and kung fu, as well as the perfect cooperation between the performers. There may be two lions dancing together briskly, and there may be

广州龙狮锦标赛现场
The scene of Guangzhou Dragon and Lion Championship

域特色的舞狮节俗，长盛不衰，历代相传。

醒狮的点睛之笔在“醒”字。狮子造型独具地方特色，威猛生动，身披鳞甲，狮头扎作玲珑精致，讲究神似，黑白相间或红绿相配，色彩鲜艳醒目，突出百兽之王的威武霸气。根据造型不同，可分为“文狮”“武狮”“七彩狮”“黑白狮”等多种类别。随着醒狮的流行，明清以来，狮头彩扎发展成一门颇具岭南地方特色的手工业。

传统舞狮讲究技巧和武术功底，也讲究整体配合，既有生动活泼的双狮表演，也有气势磅礴的多狮群舞。其中尤以表演狮子出洞、滚球、采青、上楼台等高超狮艺最具观赏性，体现了“舞”与“武”、力与美的完美融合。其中“采青”是整套狮舞的精髓，难

many lions dancing together to suggest great power. Such demanding activities as "jumping out of the cave", "rolling balls", "taking the hung gifts" and "jumping onto the platform" in the lion dance are usually very interesting and attractive, which symbolize the combination of dance and kung fu, power and beauty. "Taking the hung gifts" is the core of the lion dance and is the most difficult one, known for the beautiful movements involved, including a series of activities such as jumping, staying, swinging and falling. By the superb performance of the performers, the various emotions of the lion can be delineated or a set of stories can be told. This is the superb kung fu involved the southern lion dance.

Because of the peculiar performing skills involved and the rich connotations the dance suggests, the lion dance of Guangdong Province has become one of the cultural treasures in China. In 2006, it was listed among the national intangible cultural heritages.

Adviser of this Chapter: Jiang Mingzhi (Director and Doctoral supervisor of major of Folklore, Department of Chinese language and literature, Sun Yat-sen University)

舞狮表演 Lion dance

度高，动作美，包含起、承、转、合等过程。技艺高超的舞者，既能舞出狮子喜、怒、哀、嗔各种情绪，又能在高难度的舞狮技巧中精彩演绎一套故事，这样才真正达到南派舞狮的上乘功夫。

广东醒狮以独特的演练技巧和深厚的文化内涵，成为珍贵的中华文化瑰宝，2006年被列入国家级非物质文化遗产。

本章顾问：蒋明智（中山大学中文系民俗学教研室主任、博士生导师）

WORLD OF CUISINE
—CANTONESE DELICACY

Guangzhou cuisine is a major member of Cantonese cuisine. The advantageous geographical environment of Pearl River Delta and the inclusive Lingnan culture lead to Cantonese cuisine's reform and innovation while keeping its traditional flavor. Cantonese cuisine is one of the four major cuisines in China that include Lu cuisine, Chuan cuisine, Su cuisine and Cantonese cuisine. The saying of "born in Suzhou, living in Hangzhou, eating in Guangzhou and dying in Liuzhou" popular during the Republic of China was a summary of ideal life, and it also suggested the importance of Guangzhou food in China. Between the 1930s and the 1990s, Cantonese cuisine won a lot of awards at home and abroad, and was known all over the world.

珍味

食在广州

广州菜是粤菜的主流。珠江三角洲优越的自然地理环境、兼容并包的岭南文化特征，使粤菜在重视传承的基础上，不拘泥于传统，博采众长，善于进行改革和创新。粤菜是较早形成的“鲁、川、苏、粤”四大名菜之一。从民国时期“生在苏州，住在杭州，食在广州，死在柳州”这句概括人生理想的民谚，足见当时广州饮食在中国的地位。20世纪30年代到90年代，粤菜在国内外屡获金奖，享有很高的声誉，名扬海内外。

CANTONESE PEOPLE LOVING DELICACY

NATURE'S TREASURE

Lingnan region is located in the subtropical zone, facing South Sea. There is plenty of rain here and it is green all year round. There are also numerous lakes, bays, rivers, which produce a variety of fruits, bountiful meat, and fishes. "Any kind of food can be found in Guangdong, while Guangdong may have what you can not find in any other places." Guangdong is one of the places in China with the richest food resources.

MERGING OF THE SOUTH AND THE NORTH

In the shell mound relic of the Neolithic period at Foshan, the shells were piled up and formed a mound. This suggested that the people of the ancient Nanyue Kingdom had already began to make their living by fishing in the sea.

粤人好食

物华天宝

岭南地处亚热带，濒临南海，雨量充沛，四季常绿，湖塘星布，河流纵横，蔬果丰富，禽兽众多，河鲜琳琅，海产无数。“天下所有之食货，粤东几尽有之，粤东所有之食货，天下未必尽有也。”岭南是中国饮食资源最丰富的地区之一。

南北交汇

新石器时期佛山贝丘遗址，贝壳堆积形成山丘，说明古代越人已经以猎食海鲜为生。秦国定百越后，南越王国成立，中原文化和岭南文化交流加强。南越王墓出土用于煮汤的锅、烧烤的烤炉、煎炸的煎锅等炊器多达上百种。

及至魏晋南北朝中原频乱，宋室衰落南渡，中原汉人不断迁移到岭南，带来更加多样的中原饮食习俗。唐代广州司马刘恂在

After State Qin defeated Baiyue, the Nanyue Kingdom was founded, and the cultural communication between Central China and Lingnan region became common. The number of the pots, stoves, frying pans and other cooking utensils that were found in the tomb of the king of the Nanyue Kingdom amounts to over one hundred.

铜釜甑（zèng），广州西汉南越王博物馆藏
Copper cauldron (Nanyue King Tomb Museum of West Han Dynasty in Guangzhou)

In the chaotic period in Chinese history from A.D. 220 to 589 and Song Dynasty when the government moved to the south, the people from Central China moved to south in great numbers. They brought with them various food cultures. Liu Xun, Guangzhou governor in Tang Dynasty, recorded in his book *The Anecdotes in Lingnan* how the people in Lingnan region used tens of cooking techniques to cook food, such as boiling, roasting, frying, steaming, quick frying, braising and various seasoning materials to processing different food, such as ginger, onion, leek, pepper, and cinnamon. They were learning and developing the spirit of practicality deep in Lingnan culture. And Lingnan people incorporated the traditional cultures of Central China into Lingnan culture, which helped form the peculiar food culture in Lingnan region.

INCORPORATING OF THE EAST AND THE WEST

After the government in Tang Dynasty established an office to take care of foreign trade in Guangzhou, Guangzhou's position as the center of exportation and

铜鐎（jiāo），广州西汉南越王博物馆藏
Copper kettle (Nanyue King Tomb Museum of West Han Dynasty in Guangzhou)

《岭表录异》记载，当时岭南人熟练使用煮、炙、炸、蒸、炒、烩等十几种烹调技艺，因食物质地不同而使用生姜、葱、韭、椒、桂等各种调味料。他们在学习继承中还善于发扬岭南文化中务实创新的精神，把地方风格融入中原文化，形成岭南特有平民美食。

中西融合

唐代市舶使在广州设置后，广州作为全国外贸中心和国际海洋贸易东方中心的合法地位得到确立。“广州通海夷道”从广州启程，到达100多个国家和地区，是当时世界上最长的国际航线。宋代广州仍是通往东南亚和阿拉伯地区的主要门户，贸易发达，“所

international sea trade center in the east was settled. The trading route on the sea started from Guangzhou and reached more than 100 countries and regions in the world. It was the longest international sea route in the world at that time. Guangzhou in Song Dynasty was still the most important gate to Southeast Asia and the Arabian countries. The prosperous trading activities at that time brought into Guangzhou various flowers and fruits, animals and meats, shells and pearls, some of which could not be seen in China. The vegetables and spices imported from the other places of the world enriched the food in Guangzhou.

Guangzhou in Tang Dynasty was already an international city with foreigners and merchants from all over the world. The government delimited an area in the west part of Guangzhou for the foreigners, and there were more than 200,000 people living in this area. The food culture they brought with them merged into the local food cooking methods in Guangzhou.

As the exclusive world trading port in Qing Dynasty, Guangzhou became an important city of China in terms of economic power. The merchants from all over China gathered here, who brought with them the food culture of their hometowns. The west part of Guangzhou gathered more capital and goods where there were countless bars and restaurants. Either in summer or in winter, either in the daytime or at night, the people could enjoy delicious food there. Food cultures from the south and the north merged here, and exerted influences on Cantonese cuisine. The

鲍鱼鸡
Claypot abalone and chicken

以奇花异果，珍禽奇兽，犀珠象贝，有中州所无者”。从国外传入的蔬菜和香料，极大地丰富了粤菜的食材。

广州在唐代就是“海外藩夷，四方商贾杂居”的国际都市，朝廷在广州城西部设立的“藩区”，居住人数多达二十万人。由此带来的中外饮食文化融合大大提高了粤菜的烹饪技巧。

清代“一口通商”后，广州成为全国经济重镇，全国客商云集，也汇集八方美食，“西关尤财货之地，肉林酒海，无寒暑，亦无昼夜”，南北风味大交流，与粤菜互相影响融合。同时，十三行商人追求高端精致饮食，从海外进口昂贵的燕窝、鲍鱼、鱼翅等原材料，大厨们则不断学习、吸收各种烹饪技术，并结合本地环境、民俗、气候、口味等加以改良，使粤菜迅速发展，跻身我国四大菜系。

merchants of Shisanhang wanted to enjoy good-quality food, so they imported expensive food materials such edible swallow's nests, abalones or shark's fins. And the cooks began to learn how to cook those fancy cuisines. Based on the local environment, custom, climate, and taste, they made adaptations and innovations, and produced one of the four major cuisines in China.

FOOD VARIETY

2000 years' foreign trade armed the people of Guangzhou with a broad horizon. They became ready to absorb the food cultures from Central China and other countries while they themselves became more and more open to new things. What was inedible for the people from Central China and foreign countries became edible for the people of Guangzhou. Birds, beasts, insects, snakes, whatever they were, all became their delicacy.

Dog meat, snake meat, yellow-breasted bunting, tylorrhynchuses, cicada pupas and even water beetles become their food. Pig feet, field snails, chicken paws become the breakfast dim sum of the people of Guangzhou. And in the cold winter, a bowl of cooked bull intestines, bovine pancreas, or bull lung with turnips and seasoning materials that have been processed for four hours might call back the childhood memory of Guangzhou people.

广博杂食

两千多年的对外贸易交流，使广州人见多识广，善于广泛吸取中原和海外各国的饮食文化，也造就了广州人开放兼容的个性。在中原人、外国人眼里不能吃、不敢吃的东西，在广州人眼里正是美食，百无禁忌，不问鸟兽蛇虫，不论低档粗贱，只要经巧手烹饪，无不食之。

狗肉、蛇肉、禾花雀、禾虫、蝉蛹、龙虱备受饕餮们追捧，白云猪手、紫苏田螺、蒸凤爪是早茶名点。而在寒冷的冬天，街边吃到一碗牛肠、牛膀、牛肺加白萝卜，用花椒八角等料焖足四小时的和味牛杂，不知温暖了几代广州人的儿时记忆。

牛杂 Cooked beef offal

FOOD CHOICE

FRESHNESS

Freshness refers to the choice of fresh materials: green vegetables, fresh seafood, fresh poultry. In the years of the Republic of China, the head cooks in the big restaurants often went to the chicken fence to choose the chicken in person. If there were no satisfying materials, they would rather not cook that dishes. The hostess of the Tan family cuisine reserved a car for the whole month to allow her to go to the market to buy the fresh materials every morning. A steamed fish served on the table must have bright color, tender taste, and the meat where the fish was cut must protrude out. This always won the praise of the customers.

Freshness also means that cuisine is not too salty and the original taste of the food is kept. Take the seasoned gourd cup as an example: the ingredients like diced kidney, fresh mushroom, shrimps, lotus seeds should be boiled in the boiling water before they are put in the cooking pot

鲜字为首

“鲜”首先是指材料新鲜，蔬菜碧绿，海鲜生猛，禽类纯种。民国时各大酒家的厨师，自己去鸡栏挑鸡，当天没有满意的，宁可不做。谭家菜女主人主持私厨时，专门有包月的车供她清早出门购买时鲜。一条蒸鱼上桌，色泽光鲜、肉质滑嫩，切口部位鱼肉突

海鲜粥 Seafood porridge

so as to preserve the slight sweet taste of the white gourd. The seasoning to match the dishes is also very simple so as to foreground the original taste of the material. Other examples: boiled chicken with ginger-scallion dipping sauce; roast goose with sour plum sauce; roast suckling pig with white sugar. All are served with the meat and sauce on different dishes; the customers choose whatever they need according to their own liking. All this reflects Guangzhou people's love of freshness and their respect for the customers with their peculiar tastes.

SEASONALITY

Everything has its own season. *The Inner Canon of the Yellow Emperor* suggests that the daily diet should fit the change of the four seasons. Lingnan is rich in various natural resources, and the land here can provide food all the year round. Therefore, the people here know clearly when some food can be eaten and when not. For example, many restaurants serve a dish called "frying the seasonable vegetables", which means that different vegetables are used in the different seasons they are produced. For example, the buckwheat is cooked in spring when it tastes crisp and tender; water mustard is cooked between lunar August and the Qingming Festival the next year when it tastes sweet and crisp; the tender heart of choi sum planted in Zengcheng tastes sweet only after it is frosted; the famous dish made

八宝冬瓜盅 Seasoned waxgourd cup

起，食客们就会异口同声赞美：“这条鱼真新鲜。”

“鲜”的另一层理解是菜品的清淡。烹调时尽量保持食物本来的味道。比如著名的八宝冬瓜盅，配料肾丁、鲜菇、虾仁、莲子都先滚熟才放入，增加冬瓜的清爽甘甜。搭配菜品的调料也非常简单，起到突出菜品原味的作用。比如白切鸡配姜葱碟，烧鹅配酸梅酱，乳猪配白糖，都是小份随菜来到饭桌，不淋不浇，食客根据口味，各取所需，体现了广州人对清淡的追求和对个人口味的尊重。

不时不食

万物皆有时，《黄帝内经》提倡“司岁备物”，说的就是日常饮食要符合四时节令。岭南物产丰富，土地四季皆有所出，

增城迟菜心
The tender heart of choi sum planted in Zhengcheng

of mushroom with flowering cabbage must choose the mushrooms whose tops crack after being frosted or frozen in the cold winter, which is more tasty.

Aquatic products served on table should also be seasonable. “Spring bream, autumn carp and summer herring”, “worthless Qingming shrimp”, and “fat snakes in autumn” all tell what is the right season to eat the right food. For example, Qingming shrimp refers to the huge number of shrimp taken from the mountain rivers around Qingming Festival when it tastes solid and fresh. It is a delicacy, either boiled or fried.

ORIGINAL FLAVOR

Guangzhou people’s love of seasonable food material matches their cooking which is designed to keep the

因此广州人对“不时不食”这个原则贯彻得非常彻底。比如饭店菜牌里都能看到一道菜叫“炒时蔬”，就是指根据时节不同，用当季蔬菜烹制。如春天吃春荠，口感脆嫩，农历八月至来年清明，水东芥甜爽无渣。增城迟菜心，要打过霜才甜，名菜北菇扒菜胆，选的北菇必须是粤北地区经过寒冬霜雪自然裂出花纹的蘑菇，菇伞厚实，菇香千里。

时令的水产也有讲究。“春鳊秋鲤夏三黎”“清明虾，贱过沙”“秋风起，三蛇肥”，此等谚语，都说明了吃当季食物的美味。比如清明虾，是指清明节前后的山野河虾产量丰富，肉质结实清甜，白灼清炒都鲜美。

北菇扒菜胆　Mushrooms with flowering cabbage

original flavor of the material. For example, the Cantonese cuisine needs to be fried in iron pans quickly with violent stove fire; the quickly cooked cuisine tastes crisp, tender and juicy. To produce such a taste, first, the material must be cut neatly; second, the fire must be violent and the material in the pan must be stirred frequently to let it heated evenly; third, no extra sauce is visible while it is coated with sauce. The famous Cantonese cuisine called "sautéed water snake slice with tender vegetable" is cooked by following such steps: a snake is divided into 8 slices, then the snake slices are fried with violent stove fire; in 3 minutes, the snake slices are taken out of the pan when snake meat seems to be trembling.

Another way of cooking to keep the material's original flavor is boiling or steaming, served together with a dish of soy sauce with hot pepper slices. Only the fresh food material can be cooked by steaming, whose fresh flavor might catch the customer's heart, while a little bit extra sauce is unnecessary. The big restaurants in cities often have a big fish tank, while those in rural area seats close to a pond. Such arrangement is to guarantee that the fish taken out of the water is still fresh to keep its fresh taste.

INTEGRATION

Cantonese cuisine is characterized by its tradition regardless of its origins. The cooks often choose the food

白灼秋葵 Boiled okra

原汁原味

广州人对新鲜当季食材的追求，表现在烹饪技术上，更多地要求烹调能保持食材的原汁原味。比如粤菜小炒讲究的“镬气”就是其中之一。“镬气”是指食材在铁锅里用猛火快炒，使其快熟，保持脆爽嫩滑的口感。炒菜有镬气，一是食材切得均匀整齐；二是火猛勤抛镬，使食材受热均匀；三是勾芡要精细，打芡不见汁。出名的小炒菜远炒水蛇片，一条蛇切八片，猛火翻炒，三分钟出锅，蛇肉仿佛还在微微颤动。

另一种原汁原味的烹调方式，就是清蒸或白灼，只搭配一碟豉油辣椒圈，只有新鲜的食材才经得起清蒸的考验，仅凭自身的鲜味就能抓住食客味蕾，不需要过多酱汁来装饰。城里海鲜酒楼巨大的鱼缸、城外农家乐紧挨池塘，为的就是现捞现做，让人吃出食材最原始的鲜和美。

西施烩花肚 Braised Xishi fish maw

materials from all over the world freely to meet the demands of the customers and by the supply of the market. They take in the essence of Chinese and foreign cuisines instead of copying them. They make adaptations and innovations to produce new cuisines, which give Cantonese cuisines an everlasting new life. For example, the "new Cantonese cuisine" is a bold combination of foreign and local food materials as well as the southern and northern elements while keeping the tradition of Cantonese cuisine. Conch cooked with red wine, potato cooked with cheese, fried pig bone with mustard, fast-fried squid with XO sauce, and many other cuisines are characterized by their beautiful designs, rich tastes, and can trigger a new eating experience.

融会贯通

粤菜的特点是“有传统，无正宗”。厨师们根据市场和顾客的需要，灵活多变地大量引进世界各地的原材料，吸取中外烹调技术精华，但并不是完全复制，而是不断地移植改造，推陈出新，创造新的菜式、新的食法，使粤菜具有持续、旺盛的生命力。如“新派粤菜”，就是在传统粤菜基础上，糅合南北风味、中西风格，大胆将外国酱料与本地食材相结合，比如红酒焗花螺、芝士焗土豆、芥末炒猪仔骨、XO酱爆鲜鱿等等，卖相优雅，口感层次丰富，触发新的饮食体验。

紫苏炒田螺
Fried river snails with perilla

DIVERSE CUISINES

NINE GUI OF DELICACY

Gui was originally a round container for grains in ancient time used for sacrificing ceremonies. Nine Gui used to serve food suggests a big banquet. Guangzhou people are friendly people. The often serve eight courses with one soup for wedding ceremony, birthday party or banquet for honored guests. This is called nine gui. The courses served are not fixed, but the materials for the cuisine are usually expensive.

SLICED MEAT

Never Call It A Banquet Without Chicken

Among all the poultry materials for cussine, chicken is always indispensable. A banquet without chicken is literally not a banquet. Specially made chicken is usually the signature dish in many restaurants. The Wenchang

琳琅
菜品

九大簋：廷宴珍馐

“簋”原是古代祭祀时盛载黍稷的圆形器皿，九大簋表示宴席丰富隆重。广州人好客，在喜宴、寿宴、宴请贵宾等大型聚会上，八菜一汤的菜式，俗称“九大簋”。它的内容不是一成不变的，一般都是选较为名贵的食材烹调。

九大簋 Nine Gui Courses

chicken in Guangzhou Restaurant, the chicken cooked with Shaoxing wine in Beiyuan Restaurant, Qingping chicken in Qingping Restaurant are quite famous. The chicken can be cooked in over 20 ways, but the sliced boiled chicken is the most welcomed. The chicken to cook sliced boiled chicken must be the cage-free hens that have not laid eggs before. And the time to cook the chicken is calculated exactly by minute. The well-done sliced boiled chicken features juicy skin and tender meat, even the bones smell like chicken meat.

Colorful Cantonese Yusheng

Guangzhou people has a long history to eat yusheng, the raw fish slices feature beautiful red-white texture, thin as the cicada's wings, even they can fly up with one puff. The fish slices are put on the iced tray, decorated with shredded turnip, shredded carrot, shredded onion, shredded lemon peel, shredded ball pepper, shredded pickled koey, shredded fried taro, chopped olive nut, chopped peanuts, fried dough, cinnamon powder (used to kill the parasites), black pepper powder, sugar, salt, vinegar, and some other seasoning, looking very beautiful. All the people around the table will together take the fish slices and the seasoning up from the iced tray, symbolizing good fortune for everyone.

Sliced Roast Meat

Like sashimi, sliced roast meat also has a long history. There were already big roasting stoves in the ancient Nanyue Kingdom. Besides the most famous roast suckling

白切鲜脍：粤菜佳肴

无鸡不成宴

鸡在广州饮食中有不可替代的地位，所谓“无鸡不成宴”。酒店招牌菜里，少不了独特的招牌名鸡菜式。如广州酒家的广州文昌鸡、北园酒家的花雕鸡、清平饭店的清平鸡等等。鸡的制作方法有20多种，最出名的做法还是白切。白切鸡必须选放养的鸡（没有下过蛋的雌鸡），做白切鸡的火候精确到分钟，晚一分钟鸡肉都会过熟变老。好的白切鸡，皮爽、肉滑，吃起来骨头都有鸡味。

缤纷鱼生

广州人吃鱼生的历史很长，切鱼片到“红肌白理，轻吹可起，薄如蝉翼”的境界，放在冰盘里，搭配白萝卜丝、胡萝卜丝、洋葱丝、柠檬皮丝、甜椒丝、腌荞头、炸芋丝、榄仁碎、花生碎、薄脆、肉桂末（驱虫）、胡椒粉、糖、盐、醋等味料，色彩缤纷。吃

粤菜厨艺大赛中选手的精美刀工
The exquisite knife skills of the contestants in the Cantonese Delicacy Competition

烧腊
Sliced roast meat

pig, roast goose and roast pork are also served in slices. It is believed that the royal cook in South Song dynasty who fled with the emperor to South China taught the local people to prepare "Nanjing roast duck", and the local cooks made adaptations based on the local material and the local people's taste. They replaced the ducks with geese, designed big pots as stoves and replaced the "open roasting" with "covered roasting". Deep well roast goose was the most well known invention. During Qing Dynasty, Peking roast duck was brought to Guangdong by the government officials. The local cooks quickly learned how to roast ducks, and invented "baking stove". The baked goose features crisp crust with tender meat, and is one of the three treasures of Guangdong.

的时候众人一起动手，用公筷把调料和鱼片捞在一起，象征满桌财气福气。

惹味烧腊

烧腊和鱼生一样有历史，南越国已经有大型的铜烤炉。除了烧味之王烧乳猪，烧鹅、叉烧也是“斩料”中的重要成员。烧鹅相传是南宋随末代皇帝逃到岭南的御厨将“金陵烧鸭”的技法传给本地人。本地厨师再结合本地食材和口味进行改良，用鹅代替了鸭子，设计专门大缸，将“明炉烧”改为“暗炉烧”，发明了著名的“深井烧鹅”。清代“北京烤鸭”随南下官员传到广东，本地厨师又立刻学习技巧，摸索出“焗炉法”，使之皮脆肉嫩，成为著名的“广东三宝”之一。

深井烧鹅 Deep well roast goose

EVERYDAY LOVE

DIFFERENT METHODS OF COOKING RICE

Guangzhou people have a special love of porridge. They often use pottery or clay pots to cook porridge, so the process of cooking porridge has a term "potting porridge" (boil congee). They have a very good control on the fire when cooking porridge this way: "intense fire to boil it, slow fire to mash it; sticky in winter and spring, watery in summer and fall." Every piece of rice or millet will burst open until the water and grains melt into one. The porridge thus produced is sticky like glue with resilient texture. Based on this, Guangzhou people also invented hot fresh porridge. The well-done porridge is boiled together with other ingredients in small pots. The porridge cooked in this way is rich with different tastes. The most famous one is called "boat porridge": fish slices, fresh shrimps, shredded roast pork, fried pork skin, jellyfish, shredded ginger and chopped onion are put in a bowl, and then they pour the hot porridge in the bowl; finally some shredded fried peanuts are put on top of the

粥粉面饭

广州人对粥有不同寻常的讲究，煮粥叫“煲粥”，用瓦煲，火候要求高，“武火煲滚，文火煲透，冬春稠，夏秋稀”，米煲至粒粒开花，水米交融，出品的白粥滑稠起胶，绵而不烂。在此基础上，广州人发明了生滚粥。以白粥为底，任意选择食材，小锅滚熟，出品的粥千滋万味，鲜美可口。最著名的当属艇仔粥，生鱼片、鲜虾仁、叉烧丝、浮皮、海蛰、姜丝、葱花，一同放在碗中，用滚粥一冲而下，最后再撒上炸花生，香气扑鼻。还有状元及第

艇仔粥
Boat porridge

porridge. Besides, there is also "champion porridge": pork balls, sausage, fried pork liver and seasoning like ginger, onion are put in the porridge. Such a kind of porridge tastes fresh and slippery. Various materials that can be used to cook dishes can be put in the porridge, and we have different kinds of porridge, such as beef porridge, frog meat porridge, gingko nut and bean curd porridge.

Rice is the major crop in Lingnan region. In the old days, the local people had the tradition to grind the grains into flour to make food. Shahe rice noodle got its name because of the superb rice planted in Shanhe on the east side of Baiyuan Mountain. The noodle made of Shahe rice flour tastes resilient and slippery, and can be fried or steamed or used to make soup. The most well-known one is fried beef rice noodles. It is believed to be a dish that tests the skills of the cook, needing the cook's superb control over the fire. The materials used for this dish must be tender beef, fresh bean sprouts, and the noodles well done must be oily but dry. Another well-known food of this kind is the rice noodle roll: The rice milk is wrapped up in white cloth before it is steamed. It gets its name because the well-done noodle look like pig intestines. It is served with soy sauce and sesame oil. Later, the cook put pork, beef, shrimps and vegetables in the rice milk before it is steamed. Then the well-done rice noodle is folded three times, and the result is the new favorite in the tea houses.

A Bite of China, A Chinese documentary TV series, has once filmed the process of cooking bamboo pressed noodles. The wheat flour comes from Central China, but Guangzhou people add baking soda and duck eggs when they process the dough to fit their taste. The dough will be pressed repeatedly with

粥，粥底加入猪肉丸、粉肠、猪肝，辅以姜葱作调料，吃起来鲜美爽滑。所有能做菜的食材都可入粥，加入牛肉的牛肉粥，加入田鸡的田鸡粥，加入白果腐竹的白果粥等等，品种丰富，洋洋大观。

岭南属于稻作区，盛产大米，先民已经有研磨谷类，制作米粉食品的传统。沙河粉，因原产于白云山东麓的沙河镇得名。沙河粉口感柔韧爽滑，煎炒蒸烫无一不能，最出名的是干炒牛河，传闻是考验厨师水平高低的一道硬菜，对火候和兜炒技术要求很高，必须是牛肉鲜嫩，豆芽爽口，粉条油润干身，才算成功的干炒牛河。另一种出名的是猪肠粉，因米浆在白布隔水蒸熟，卷成猪肠形状得名，配豉油、芝麻食用。后来大厨在米浆里加入猪肉、牛肉、虾仁等和蔬菜一起蒸熟，再将肠粉从布上拉起来折三下，成为茶楼里的新宠布拉肠。

《舌尖上的中国》拍摄过竹升面的制作过程。小麦粉来自中原，但广州人在和面时根据地方口味，加入少量碱水和鸭蛋，揉后用特制大竹升反复压制数个小时，面吃起来有韧劲，带着蛋香。

煲仔饭是广州特有街头美食。广州的瓦煲，刷油，放入泡好的

煲仔饭
Claypot Rice

specially-made bamboo sticks for several hours. The noodles made this way taste resilient and have the taste of duck eggs.

Potted rice is a special kind of food that can be seen on the streets in Guangzhou. The pottery or clay pot peculiar to Guangzhou will be used to make this kind of food. To make potted rice, the pot is coated with oil first, and the rice that is soaked through with water is put into the pot, then intense fire is used until the water in the pot is boiling, then the well-prepared materials are put in the pot when it is half done, then slow fire is used until almost all the water has evaporated, and finally chopped onion and hot oil are put onto the rice. The rice made this way is very delicious. The most traditional rice is the potted rice cooked with cured meat. Cured duck meat, liver sausage, meat sausage and cured pork are mixed with the oily rice. No one can resist the rice cooked this way. When all the rice is eaten, you can also taste the crisp golden rice crust at the bottom of the pot. It is also delicious.

广州虾饺皇
Shrimp dumplings of Guangzhou

TWO-SNACKED TEA

Guangzhou people often say, "Let's drink tea when we're free." The tea here is the tea served in a tea houses. Tea house in Guangzhou has a long history that can be traced back to the tea provided for the public to enjoy their free time in Qing Dynasty. Tea house appeared in the late years of Qing Dynasty where both tea and snacks were

大米，用猛火煮开，文火慢焖，待饭七八成熟，放入备好的食材，小火细焗，水尽饭成，开盖撒葱花浇入熟油，芳香扑鼻。最传统的是腊味煲仔饭，腊鸭、肝肠、肉肠、腊肉四种腊味组合，油脂混合米饭的热量，开盖已经令人垂涎欲滴。煲仔饭吃到最后还有“彩蛋”，那便是煲底焦黄脆香的锅巴，入口酥脆，滋味悠长。

一盅两件

广州人有句口头禅：“得闲饮茶。”这个茶就是茶楼的茶。茶楼在广州的历史悠久，可以追溯到清代供普罗大众休息的茶居，晚清出现茶楼，提供茶水，也卖点心。最初的“一盅两件”，“盅”指的是一碗盖茶，“两件”指的是蒸包和炒米饼两种点心。但发展到当代，茶器精致，点心多达上万款，代表作有虾饺、烧卖、炸春卷、炸芋角、马蹄糕、鸡蛋盏、萝卜糕和肉肠粉等等。

茶点 Tea snacks

served. At the beginning, what was served is a cup of tea served in a cup with a lid and two snacks. One snack was the steamed bread with fillings, and the other one fried rice cake. Today, the tea cup becomes more exquisite, and thousands of snacks can be served. The most favorite snacks include shrimp dumplings, steamed dumplings, fried spring rolls, fried potato chips, horse-hoof-like cake, egg cups, turnip cake, sausage rice noodles, etc.

红米肠 Red rice sausage

NOURISHING SOUP AND LOCAL DRINKS

It is humid and hot in Lingnan region. The way for the people here to cope with this humid and hot climate is to eat soup. The people here have to tolerate the humid and hot or dry weather and might suffer from excessive internal heat inside their bodies. Guangzhou people studied the different nature of different food materials that might have different effects on human bodies. They use these different types of materials to cook soup.

To avoid humidity and heat, in summer they cook nourishing, light and cooling soup, or pearl barley soup with white gourd and duck. To cope with the cold winter, they cook soup with pig stomachs and black pepper, or with American ginseng and black-boned chicken, to make one feel warm in the stomach and help avoid internal dryness. The so-called "boiling three and stewing four" refers to the time used to cook soup. The well-chosen materials, after

好汤好水

岭南地区湿度大、气温高，人们对付潮湿闷热气候的办法就是煲汤。针对湿热、上火、干燥等不同情况，广东人研究食材本身清、凉、温、寒的不同特质，搭配煲制多种类型的汤。比如盛夏会煲清补凉、冬瓜老鸭薏米汤这类清热去湿的汤，而秋冬则会煲胡椒猪肚、花旗参炖竹丝鸡这类驱寒暖胃、滋阴润燥的老火汤。所谓"三煲四炖"，说的是汤的熬制时间。精选食材，经过慢火细煲（炖），耐心地等候食材把自身的精华一点一点融入汤里，汤汁浓郁，润人心肺。

对付暑湿天气，广东人还有另外两件法宝：凉茶和糖水。凉茶不是茶叶，而是各类具有解表、解感、润燥、化湿作用的中草药。如清热解毒喝菊花茶、金银花茶，感冒喝板蓝根，咳嗽喝冰糖雪耳……土生土长的广东人，说起凉茶，每个人都能发表独特见解。

老火清补凉汤
Double boiled cooling & Nourishing soup

the long-time boiling or stewing, could release the essence of their nutrition in the soup. The sticky soup always makes the locals feel happy.

To cope with the humidity in summer, Guangzhou people invented another two magic cooking methods: herbal tea and syrup. Herbal tea is not the traditional tea as we understand, but a kind of Chinese herbal medicine that functions to deal with fever, internal heat and internal dampness. To remove internal heat and toxicity, they drink chrysanthemum flower tea, or honeysuckle flower tea; to cure fever, they drink water soaking isatis root; to cure coughing, they drink syrup made of rock candy and snow pear...Any native Guangdong people know what herbal tea means to them.

Shops selling syrup often stand side by side with shops selling herbal tea. Herbal tea tastes bitter, while syrup tastes sweet. The syrup in Guangzhou is the health-preserving delicacy used also to avoid heat. It is often made with water and rock candy. There are a great variety of syrup: syrup with seaweed and mung bean, or syrup with waternut, lilium brownie root and lotus seed, or mung bean paste used to keep cool in summer; tendril-leaved fritillary bulb cooked with snow pear, or papaya cooked with transparent white fungus to be eaten in autumn; sesame porridge to be eaten in winter to keep one healthy. Many famous brands of syrup were often sold in some remote lanes of Guangzhou. Visitors often need a local guide to find the best and authenlic syrup.

Adviser of this Chapter: Zhou Songfang (Expert in Lingnan culture and history, Adjunct research professor of Institute of Ancient Literature, Sun Yat-sen University)

川贝炖雪梨
Tendril-leaved fritillary bulb cooked with snow pear

糖水铺紧挨着凉茶铺，凉茶味苦，糖水多甜。广东的糖水实际上是养生甜品，同样用消暑滋补的食材，加水和冰糖熬制。糖水品种繁多，祛暑有海带绿豆糖水、马蹄百合莲子糖水、绿豆沙，秋天干燥喝川贝炖雪梨、木瓜炖银耳，冬天喝芝麻糊，可以滋阴壮阳。许多招牌糖水铺，都藏在老街小巷，必须有本地人带领，才能吃到物美价廉的正宗糖水。

本章顾问：周松芳（岭南文史专家，中山大学古文献所兼职研究员）

AFTERWORD

Lingnan culture: Youth Book will be published soon. In the process of compiling this book, we cooperated with Nanfang Daily Press, and we referred frequently to the studies of the scholars about Lingnan painting, Cantonese music, Cantonese opera, Lingnan architecture, Lingnan customs and Cantonese delicacy. We especially referred to *Books of Panyu Culture* published by Sun Yat-sen University Press, and we thank those experts and advisers and many others for their precious help.

We hope the readers can benefit from this book, which will help them love their motherland much more and foster a stronger sense of identity of Lingnan culture that is so open, pragmatic, inclusive and innovative. So they can spread the Lingnan culture further and bring it to a new height of development.

May this city give her people sweet memories! May the people here always remember her!

October 2019

后 记

《岭南文化青年读本》这本小书今将付梓。在编写此书的过程中，我们与南方日报出版社通力合作，查阅了大量专家学者关于岭南画派、广东音乐、粤剧、岭南建筑、岭南民俗和粤菜方面的书籍与研究成果，借鉴参考了中山大学出版社编辑的《番禺文化丛书》，得到本书顾问团队多位专家学者的指点与帮助，汇集多方心血，在这里深表感谢。

希望读者能在阅读之后有所裨益，对脚下的这片土地和开放、务实、兼容、创新的岭南文化有更多认同感，成为岭南文化的传播者，使岭南文化发扬光大。

让城市留下记忆，让人们记住乡愁。

2019年10月